DETECTIVE W

"Help me down," said Hannah

DETECTIVE WORZEL GUMMIDGE

Barbara Euphan Todd

Illustrations by Jill Crockford

A TARGET BOOK
published by
the Paperback Division of
W. H. Allen & Co. Ltd

A Target Book
published in 1978 by the Paperback Division of
W. H. Allen & Co. Ltd
A Howard & Wyndham Company
44 Hill Street, London W1X 8LB

First published in Great Britain by
Evans Brothers Ltd, 1963

To Frances Emma Walker with love

Printed in Great Britain by
Richard Clay (The Chaucer Press), Ltd., Bungay, Suffolk

ISBN 0 426 20015 2

Contents

Illustrations

I
Detective Robin

It was a dry and windy spring morning. Straws were blowing from the cottage thatches. Outside Scatterbrook Post Office, Marlene Snooks was writing her name in the dust. She was using the toe of her sandal, and working so hard that she did not notice Robin who, hands in pockets, was scuffling his way along the village street. He did not see her either because his head was bent, and he was staring down at the litter of dust and straw and sweet-papers that had blown to the side of the pavement.

Half a minute later, the children's heads collided.

"Look where you're going!" said Marlene, rubbing her forehead.

"I *am* looking where I'm going—that's just what I am doing."

"If you *had* been looking you'd have seen me."

Robin straightened himself, put a hand to his forehead, and muttered, "I wasn't looking for you: I was looking for clues. I'm being a detective."

"What sort of clues?"

"Murderers' mostly, and burglars'."

"Has there been a murder in Scatterbrook?"—

Marlene's eyes shone with excitement—"a real murder with BLOOD?"

"Well, there might be any time, and if I found the clue, I'd cop the chap. In books," Robin spoke contemptuously, "in books the 'tecs look for the clues after the crimes have been done, and they waste bags of time. I'm going to be a very special sort of 'tec—I'll have the clues ready BEFORE the crime and fit the chap to them."

"What chap?" enquired Marlene.

"The criminal chap, of course—the murderer or the gangster or the robber-with-violence."

Robin swooped down, scrabbled in the dust, scooped up a Coca-Cola bottle-top, and wrapped it in his handkerchief.

Marlene used her latest expression, "What's that in aid of?"

"Well, if there's been a murder and the murderer had bought Coke at the Post Office, he'd have left a finger-print on the bottle-top, and then the police'd take *his* finger-prints, and they'd match the ones on the bottle-top. See?"

Marlene shook her head. "I can't see our Mr Wilson" (he was the Scatterbrook policeman), "I can't see Freddy Wilson taking finger-prints from everyone that's bought Coke at the Post Office."

"If he was smart he would, and then I'd have the print on the bottle-top, and they'd match."

"I call that silly!" argued Marlene, "Lots of people buy Coke, and they can't all be murderers."

Robin scarcely heard her, because he had drifted into a private dream—*I'll be like one of those boys who remember the numbers of cars—cars full of bank robbers, and be thanked and given gold watches by Mayors, and patted on the back by magistrates. And when I'm grown up I'll go to Scotland*

Yard and be the best detective. And nobody will dare to stop me when I ride bikes without lights on footpaths. (Lately he had been warned by P.C. Wilson for committing those offences.)

"They can't all be murderers," repeated Marlene, "not *all* the people who buy Coke at the Post Office."

She was spoiling Robin's game, and quite sensibly too, because there was truth in her argument.

"It's not only finger-prints," he muttered, "it's car numbers and footprints and—and writing names in dust. F'rinstance if Mrs Bloomsbury-Barton had been murdered in the Post Office, and I came along and saw your name written in the dust after you'd run away, I'd know, wouldn't I?"

"Know what?" asked Marlene, but she smoothed the dust with the sole of her right sandal until no trace of her name remained.

"I'd know you'd done the murder."

"Not if other people had been in the Post Office."

"But I know you don't like Mrs Bloomsbury-Barton."

Marlene scuffled out the full stop that came after her name. This detective game was beginning to be rather frightening. She spoke abruptly: "I think I'll start collecting bottle-tops: they might come in useful one day. I could string them on wires and polish them up and sell them to people to scare the birds off their peas."

In her father's loft, Marlene, who was a jackdaw of a child, had a great collection of things that "might come in useful one day." She kept broken china and string and lengths of wire, bent nails, half-empty paint tins and every shape of box.

"You can give me that bottle-top as a start."

Robin clutched the handkerchief tightly.

"All right, meanie!"

Marlene turned away to read the notices on the board by the Post Oflce door. They were very interesting. Miss Dollit wanted to sell some gramophone records. Mrs Bloomsbury-Barton wished to buy half a dozen pullets "on the point of lay." Armchairs, an electric cooker, perambulators, a child's bicycle and some bee-hives were offered for sale.

"Wish I'd a lot of money," sighed Marlene, "then I'd buy them all, and start a shop, and then——" She broke off, and pointed to a notice.

CONTRIBUTIONS ARE REQUIRED FOR A CHILDREN'S HOLIDAY TREAT. GIFTS OF CAKES, JAM, JELLIES AND ANYTHING SUITABLE FOR TEA SHOULD BE BROUGHT TO THE WHITE HOUSE NOT LATER THAN 11 A.M. ON SATURDAY APRIL 6TH.

"Look!" said Marlene. "Mrs Bloomsbury-Barton's giving a party, and she's not asked us."

"She will," muttered Robin, "and it'll mean Sunday clothes."

"It'll mean a grand tea, and lots of bottle-tops for my collection, and ices, and a sweet scramble."

Robin grunted. He was reading another notice that was much more interesting to him. Miss Dollit had lost a black-and-white kitten, and was offering five shillings reward for its return.

An arm in a flowery sleeve, a hand, holding a fountain-pen, was thrust between the children's heads, and the voice of Mrs Bloomsbury-Barton exclaimed, "Ah! Robin and Marlene! You are the little people I particularly want to see."

"Good morning, Mrs Bloomsbury-Barton."

Marlene had answered in her most polite voice. She smirked happily as she waited for the invitation that must surely come. Even an iced lolly would not have melted in her mouth. Robin grinned, too. After all, the holidays were dragging a little, and the thought of a party tea was pleasant.

"Wait a moment, my dears; don't run away." Mrs Bloomsbury-Barton clicked her tongue against the roof of her mouth. "Dear! Dear! Just as I thought—Miss Dollit has forgotten to write that the children for whom the treat is being given are coming from the Sunnyfield Orphanage—poor little things!"

Her fountain-pen spluttered as she added some words to the notice.

"Now then." She turned to Robin and Marlene. "We are having tea and an Easter Egg Hunt for the mites from the Orphanage, and I want you children to help to paint them."

Memories of a history lesson crept into Robin's mind.

"All over?" he asked. "All over like ancient Britons with woad or——"

Marlene, who had shared the history lesson, and who knew that ancient Britons had stained themselves with the juice of a plant called woad, though it was a silly thing to do, interrupted. "I've lots of blue-bags with bits of blue left in them. We could squeeze the blue into buckets of water and——"

"And dip the orphans like sheep!" added Robin, thinking that this would be a glorious game.

"Don't be silly!" Mrs Bloomsbury-Barton spoke crushingly; and then she explained her plan.

Mrs Braithewaite, the farmer's wife, had promised several dozen eggs, which were to be hard-boiled, and painted in bright colours. Miss Dollit was to arrange an Easter Egg Hunt on Saturday afternoon before tea.

"And," added Mrs Bloomsbury-Barton, "Mrs Braithewaite is lending the old dairy for this afternoon, and I want you to help paint the eggs. We shall expect you punctually at two o'clock."

"We could paint faces on the eggs," said Marlene.

"Now, that is a very good idea," agreed Mrs Bloomsbury-Barton. "On Easter Sunday, you will be able to think of the dear little orphans enjoying hard-boiled eggs for breakfast—hard-boiled eggs with pretty, painted faces. Two o'clock punctually this afternoon, children, and don't forget to bring your paint-boxes. Now I must fly."

She did not exactly fly, but, as she bustled down the road, she looked just a little like a fussy hen.

"I *was* going to have been a detective this afternoon," complained Robin. "I've never heard of a 'tec painting eggs for orphans."

Marlene spoke wisely, "If we don't paint eggs we mayn't be asked to the party."

"Who wants parties that interrupt plans?"

Robin turned to the notice-board, saw that Mrs Marble had found a pair of spectacles in the churchyard, and that Major Wazenby-Gunthorpe had lost a latchkey.

"A burglar could pick that up," he muttered, "and then he could burgle the house it belongs to. I ought to find the key before the burglar does. I could put it on a path where a burglar could see it. I'd hide behind a tree till he came along and picked it up. Then I'd follow him, and see which house he burgled, and——"

"If it was Major Wazenby-Gunthorpe's key, it would be Major Wazenby-Gunthorpe's house," interrupted Marlene.

There was a long silence; then Robin answered triumphantly, "It mightn't be. Major Wazenby-Gunthorpe might have pinched the key from—from Mrs Kibbins, and be wanting to burgle her cottage."

"Mrs Kibbins hasn't got a latchkey—her key's as big as the church door key!"

"He might have pinched Mrs Bloomsbury-Barton's key, and lost it before he could start burgling."

"Likely!" scoffed Marlene. "That's *very* likely!"

"It's the unlikely people that are criminals at the end. All 'tecs know that!"

"You needn't tell me that Major Wazenby-Gunthorpe would burgle Mrs Bloomsbury-Barton."

"He might be innocent, then, but his finger-prints would be on the key and he'd be suspected. If I followed the real burglar, I'd save Major Wazenby-Gunthorpe from prison and be rewarded."

"Major Wazenby-Gunthorpe's a magistrate. He sends people to prison—he doesn't go there."

"That's all *you* know!" said Robin. "Besides——"

The argument was interrupted by the slamming of the Post Office door, which meant that the time was one o'clock.

"We'll be late for our dinners!" exclaimed Marlene. "We'll never be in the old dairy by two o'clock at this rate."

As a matter of fact, the children did not reach the farm until a great deal later. This was partly because they met their second favourite scarecrow in the stackyard.

"Oh, my dears," said Earthy Mangold, clasping her twiggy fingers till they crackled, "I'm in such a taking! Have you found him?"

"Found who?" asked Marlene, though she might have guessed that Earthy Mangold was referring to her husband, Worzel Gummidge, who was the most important of all the Scatterbrook scarecrows.

"Mr Gummidge. I keeps on missin' him. I've missed him horrible since he went away three days ago."

"Which way did he go?" asked Robin.

"I casn't say that acos I shut my eyes so's not to see the last of him."

Green tears trickled down Earthy's potato-face. "I never can abear to see folks goin' away and gettin' smaller and smaller. It's not nice bein' a wife to someone as looks as little as a standin' up earwig. It makes you ashamed to be keepin' on so big. If I'd walked alongside o' him, we'd have kept the same size."

"Why didn't you?" asked Marlene. "Were you quarrelling?"

Earthy shook her head, then nodded it, so that a shower of green tears spattered her blue checked apron and spangled her sacking cloak.

"I don't rightly know. They say it takes two to make a quarrel, but Mr Gummidge seems to manage on his own. Ever so wild he talked about not being pestered by *little* nests takin' up his pocket room, and not havin' to keep standin' still and standin' up while they fetched and carried."

"While who fetched and carried?" asked Marlene.

"He didn't happen to mention their names."

Robin straddled his legs, put his hands into the pockets of his shorts, and boasted, "I'll soon find Worzel Gummidge now that I'm a detective."

"What's a teckative?" asked Earthy.

It was difficult to explain about clues and finger-prints and footmarks to the little scarecrow. She looked more and more puzzled every moment, especially when Robin suggested that her scarecrow husband might have lost his memory, and added, "then he wouldn't know who he was!"

"But he'd only have to look at his bottle-straw boots and his broomstick legs and his tarred-string braces. There's no other scarecrow dresses so smart as Mr Gummidge. He'd only have to look at the hole in the side of his hat."

"He wouldn't be able to see his hat!" argued Marlene. "He couldn't see his hat if he was wearing it."

Earthy answered proudly: "His hat takes on and off same as his other clothes'd do if he demeaned himsel' to moult. Very perlite Mr Gummidge is. He allus takes his hat off to show to ladies, same as Mr Braithewaite does. It were a habit as were very disturbin' to the father robin when he happened to be perchin' on top o' his hat when he were showin' it to ladies."

Robin gave a sudden shout. "I've got it. I've got a clue. I bet you anything that Gummidge is standing on his head somewhere so that the robins can't nest in his coat-pocket. That's what he's doing!"

Earthy wrinkled the potato skin of her forehead because she was so puzzled. Little trickles of earth ran down from their furrows to make mud with the remaining green tears on her cheeks.

"That don't seem sensible, love. Mr Gummidge'd have to have bendy legs if he were to stand on his head. He'd need barrel-hoop legs afore he could do that. Mr Gummidge has broomsticks."

"No, he wouldn't. *My* legs aren't barrel-hoops. I'll show you!"

He took a run, somersaulted, landed on his hands, propped his legs against a hay-rick and lowered his head to the ground. In imitation, Marlene turned a few cartwheels, and stood upright.

"There you see!" panted Robin, whose near-to-the-ground face was nearly as red as his hair. "There you see! I bet that's what Gummidge is doing, so that robins can't nest in his coat-pocket!"

Earthy burst into another flood of green tears, and sobbed chokingly, "If he's doin' that the robins'll nest in his trousey legs, and he'll have to stay like that till the young 'uns is hatched. I casn't abear to have an upside-down-husbin! Asides, there's a hole in his hat. Mice'd nest in his hat, and mice is terrible restless. If that's a clue, it's not a nice kind one—it's not nice at all."

Robin righted himself, and pulled some straws out of his hair.

Marlene giggled because cart-wheeling had made her feel dizzy and silly. "P'raps he's building his own nest. P'raps he's laying Easter eggs!"

Earthy looked at her reprovingly.

"He'd not demean hisel'; Mr Gummidge is a he-scarecrow. I happened to have a lady friend scarecrow as thought she *had* laid eggs. Ever so pleased she were. She happened to have had a lay-down in a medder by a stream, and she happened to have a nest-shaped stummick—all bits o' sticks and hay, stickin' out untidy-like where her skin'd frayed away.

"When she came-to arter her lay-down, she happened to see an egg lyin' in the middle o' her stummick that happened to be like a nest. Highly delighted she were, and she stayed still so's not to addle the egg. Stood to reason she couldn't sit on it acos her stummick were in the wrong place, but she put her hands over it at night to keep it warm. She happened to have oven-glove hands which were cosy. At sunrise, she shook the dew off of her hands so's the sun could warm the egg. She lay there, feelin' hopeful, and dreamin' about a scarecrow-hatch. While she were hopin', a moorhen come along and settled on the nest.

" 'Well now, isn't that kind?' she thought, 'Isn't that kind and comfortin': the moorhen's goin' to hatch my egg for me?'

"She lay there, thinkin' happy thoughts, and arter a bit, the moorhen got up and jerked its tail at her, and skedaddled off into the stream. Then my friend—her name were Bossy Coot—saw there was another egg layin' along o' the first 'un."

"Had the moorhen laid them both?" asked Marlene.

"Bossy Coot weren't sure about that, acos she weren't a very noticin' lady," replied Earthy. "If she *had* happened to be a noticin' lady she'd have noticed if she'd laid the eggs hersel. She went on havin' a lay-down till there was seven eggs on her stummick. Then she went on havin' another lay down for three weeks while the moorhen sat on the eggs. Grass grew up through the holes in her oven-glove hands. She went on hopin' and dreamin' about the seven little scarecrows as'd hatch out. She kept worritin' for fear they'd not be able to peck their way through the shells. She passed the time away thinkin' grateful thoughts about the moorhen for bein' so kind as to sit on the eggs. And she passed more time away wonderin' if the little scarecrows'd hatch out ready dressed or in their sticks, and then—and then——"

Earthy's voice trembled. "And then the moorhen got up and jerked its tail at her, and seven baby moorhens scrabbled out o' the nest, and followed their mum into the water. It weren't only the disappointment as Bossy Coot minded—it were the way the moorhen acted, so deceitful and cuckoo-like, and not a word o' thanks for the loan o' the stummick nest."

As Earthy finished her story, Marlene whispered, "Mrs Bloomsbury-Barton's just coming out of the old dairy."

"Let's hide!" breathed Robin, but it was too late.

"Children! Children!" called Mrs Bloomsbury-Barton, and as they reached her she spoke sorrowfully. "This is rather disappointing. A certain little girl and a certain little boy should be hard at work by now. Come along quickly, and make up for lost time."

"But we've got to find someone first," objected Robin.

"You can play hide-and-seek another day," Mrs Bloomsbury-Barton told him.

Slowly, because they could hear the sad sighing of Earthy Mangold, Robin and Marlene went into the old dairy.

2

Detective Gummidge

THE OLD DAIRY (far superior to the shining new one—at least in the eyes of children) was a pleasant place. It was white-washed, and because it was not used nowadays except as a kind of store-room, spiders' webs made grey and lacy curtains in the corners of the windows.

A collection of battered churns, looking like the jars for Ali-Baba's thieves, stood at one end of the room.

A 'tec could hide in one of those, thought Robin. *He could hide there with a lid over his head, and then jump out and catch a milk-thief.*

Wonder if Mrs Braithwaite would spare me an old churn, thought Marlene. *An old churn would come in useful for lots of things. I could sell it to the gipsies on the Downs. They haven't any baths in the caravans, but they could pop their children in and out of a churn full of water. A churn would be worth a lot to a gipsy.*

There was a long, scrubbed table in the middle of the dairy. Round it and sitting on benches were half a dozen Scatterbrook schoolchildren. Some were licking their paint brushes: others were painting faces on eggs.

A primus stove stood on a grey slate slab under one of the windows. Beside it, her sleeves rolled up, Miss Dollit was spooning eggs into a pan of boiling water.

Mrs Braithewaite was taking more eggs from a basket, and arranging them on a rack.

Robin plumped himself down beside Queenie Simmonds because he noticed that she had a big tube of yellow paint, and he had decided to paint Chinamen gangsters' faces on his eggs.

"That's mine!" said Queenie. "You can't have that tube. I'm going to give all my faces lots and lots of yellow hair. They'll have golden hair and pink cheeks and blue eyes."

"Soppy sort of faces!" grunted Robin. "O.K.! Keep your old yellow. I'll paint thugs' faces on *my* eggs, and clues at the back—black finger-prints and red footmarks to show the murderers have been treading in blood!"

"Land's sake!" exclaimed Mrs Braithewaite. "Do you want to scare the poor little orphans into fits?"

Marlene began to paint the face of a ginger kitten. Her brush went into her mouth almost as often as it went on to the eggshell: that was because a kittens' whiskers are fine and fiddly things, and she needed a sharp point to the brush. One of the kitten's eyes was higher than the other. Its nose, which should have been pink, turned to bright crimson. It was a perfect nightmare of a kitten.

Tell you what, thought Marlene to herself. *Kittens are too difficult. I'll paint a Worzel Gummidge face on the next egg and I'll give it to Earthy Mangold as a keepsake, it'll be as good as a snapshot. I'll paint Hannah Harrow* (she was the invalid scarecrow, and had tarred bootlaces for hair, and suffered from mice, because she had been stuffed with the sawdust from a greengrocer's shop) *with her shawl. I'll paint Mildew Turmut* (she was the Railway Scarecrow, who had red and green flags for hands, and who wore the strap from a railway carriage window as a belt) *I'll paint Upsidaisy* (she was the school-allotment scarecrow. She had milking-stool legs. Her hands were woollen gloves stuffed with paper) *in her sailor hat.*

It was a busy and, for a time, quite a peaceful scene. Red heads (Robin's was the reddest), golden heads and brown heads bent over the paint boxes, brushes dipped in and out of water. Tongues became blue and green and brown and yellow from brush-licking, and there was the sound of heavy breathing.

Recklessly, Robin smashed an egg, and tried to use the yolk instead of yellow paint, but he was not very successful because the hard-boiled yolk would neither run nor powder. He decided to turn the rest of his eggs into the heads of policemen. *They'll be easy,* he thought. *They'll be easy because the pointed ends of eggs are helmet-shaped.*

The trouble was that he had no indigo paint, and neither had his neighbours.

"I can mix cobalt and black," he muttered, "that should make a fine navy blue."

He turned to Queenie Simmonds, who had found a scrap of looking glass, and was painting her own lips vermilion. She was a little girl, who loved winning prizes, and being Queen of the May, and presenting bouquets to ladies who opened bazaars. She wore her hair in tight plaits so that it could be frizzed out at any moment.

"Please," said Robin. "Please will you lend me that tube of cobalt blue."

"I want it for blue eyes. I'm painting princesses."

"You're not: you're painting your mouth."

Queenie simpered "I *am* painting a princess. Gran calls me her little princess—that's because Mum's name's Queen, too. And I'm going to paint lots of blue eyes."

"You can't want all that blue for little niggly eyes!" argued Robin.

"You can have my rose-madder if you like."

"Whoever saw a policeman in a rose-madder helmet?"

"I think it would look smart."

Mrs Bloomsbury-Barton was talking to Miss Dollit, who was shaking an egg-timer. Mrs Braithewaite was talking to both of them, and sorting eggs at the same time. All three grown-ups had their backs turned to the table, and Robin saw his chance. He grabbed Queenie's paint box and, not on purpose but because he was in a hurry, upset a jar of muddy painting water into the lap of her clean mauve frock.

There was a yell. Queenie jumped up, and shouted, "I'll tell my mum, Robin Elliot, and she'll make your mum buy me a new frock."

The grown-ups crowded round, and Marlene, who had finished painting a Gummidge face on to a brown egg, saw her chance, and slipped out of the dairy.

Earthy was standing where the children had left her. She was staring sadly up at the sky as though hoping that Worzel Gummidge would drop from it.

"Hullo!" said Marlene.

"Have you found Mr Gummidge?" asked Earthy, and she stopped gazing at the sky, though a long wriggly streak left by a passing aeroplane shone like a silver pencil mark across the cloudless blue.

"No; we've not had time yet—we've been painting hen eggs for orphans. We've been painting faces on them."

"I oncst saw some orphan lambs, but they'd faces o' their own—one was black and t'other white."

"I mean," said Marlene patiently, "I mean we've been painting faces on the eggs."

"Beggin' your pardon, then, and if it's all the same to you I'd a thought it were more important to look for

Mr Gummidge than to paint faces on the outside o' eggs that'll have the faces comin' out o' their insides. Asides, if hens wanted their eggs painted, they could paint 'em theirsels."

"But they couldn't," argued Marlene. "I don't think they could." She wondered if an artist-hen would use a tail or a wing-tip or if it would hold a paint brush in its beak.

"Beggin' your pardon, and if it's all the same to you I oncst saw a hen as had fluttered into a pot o' green paint. Then it flew on to a clothes-line, and shook itsel. Arter that, all Mrs Briggs' childers' clothes looked like they was covered with greenfly—ever so pretty they were."

Marlene took the egg out of her pocket and held it till it was level with Earthy Mangold's face.

"There!" she said, "I've done a painting of Worzel Gummidge. You can keep it to remind you of him."

Earthy was not to be comforted. Indeed, the sight of the Gummidgy face on the egg distressed her very much.

"I knew as he's gone small!" she sobbed. "I told you I seed him goin' smaller and smaller as he walked away from me. Now he's not got no broomstick arms and legs neither."

Marlene tried to explain that paintings of people were not so big as the people, or very seldom.

"Nobody," she said. "Nobody could paint a house as big as a house, there wouldn't be enough paper."

"I've seen house-painters workin'," Earthy told her. "I've seen 'em paintin' Mrs Bloomsbury-Barton's house, and that were just the same size when they'd finished. I've seen Mr Dyke paintin' Mr Braithewaite's gates, an' they stayed the same size. If they'd not stayed the same size cows could a stepped over 'em."

It is very very difficult to argue with a scarecrow, and

Marlene stopped trying. She wrapped the egg in Earthy Mangold's banana skin handkerchief, and stuffed it into the pocket of the blue-checked apron.

"Ooh aye!" said Earthy. "Stands to reason——"

Marlene interrupted excitedly, "You said that like Mr Gummidge! You said, 'Ooh aye! Stands to reason!' just like he does!"

"Ooh aye!" agreed Earthy. "Stands to reason I've got to talk to mysel same as Mr Gummidge'd talk to me if he were alongside; and stands to reason things has got to be painted same size as the things or we'd have bee-hives as big as cottages, and churches the size o' mole-hills. Thankee for the egg, my dear. Maybe it'll hatch out if I keep it cosy."

"Goodbye!" said Marlene, who had not the heart to tell Earthy that the egg was hard-boiled. Nor had she the time, or she would be scolded for having run away from the old dairy.

The other children were painting, but not so busily, when she returned to her place at the big table. Mrs Braithewaite, Mrs Bloomsbury-Barton and Miss Dollit were chatting in a corner. Queenie was glaring at Robin.

Marlene picked up her brush, and began to dab blue spots on to a brown egg because she was tired of painting faces.

Like many other occupations, painting is great fun to begin with, but as soon as blots drip from brushes, and edges are smeared and lines go crooked, interest is lost—especially on a fine afternoon in spring.

Marlene yawned loudly, and because yawning is one of the most infectious things in the world. Norma, who was sitting beside her, yawned, too; so did Billy and Henry and Shirley.

I'll paint a yawn, thought Robin, *an egg's sort of yawn-shaped. I'll paint a lip at the top and a lip at the bottom and a tongue and teeth in between.*

Mrs Bloomsbury-Barton, who had heard the yawns, turned round, clapped her hands for silence, and said, "I don't think we are *all* working quite so hard as we might. There will be two prizes—one for the child who paints the prettiest faces and another for the child who paints the greatest number of eggs."

At once, paint brushes were sloshed into water, and dots squiggles, stripes and stars appeared on eggs that had been so neat and pretty and soft-coloured when they lay in their nests.

"Gently! Gently! More haste, less speed!" said Mrs Bloomsbury-Barton. Don't forget that if a thing is worth doing, it is worth doing well!"

Miss Dollit shook her spoon, and declared, "We shall soon run out of eggs!"

The words made Marlene giggle as she imagined lots of tiny Miss Dollits in skirts and twin-sets and beads, and lots of tiny Mrs Bloomsbury-Bartons in flowery frocks and hats, and several tiny Mrs Braithewaites in blue aprons and with their sleeves rolled up, all running out of eggs from the nests of bewildered hens.

Mrs Braithewaite said loudly. "One or two of the children might go round the farmyard and look for eggs; some of the hens are sure to have laid this afternoon."

At once, every child in the room stood up, and there were shouts of "I'll go! Let me!"

"Only one or two, please," said Mrs Braithewaite, "I don't want a whole crowd of children rushing about in the barns."

"Shall we send Queenie?" suggested Miss Dollit kindly.

"It will be a sort of consolation prize for her. I mean it will make up for having had paint-water splashed on her frock. What do you think, Mrs Braithewaite?"

"I don't mind which children go, so long as they don't disturb the sitty-hen in the coop. Her chicks should hatch out in another three days."

"Queenie, then," agreed Mrs Bloomsbury-Barton, "Queenie and Robin."

Mrs Braithewaite handed a basket to Queenie.

"Off you go!" she said "There's bound to be some eggs in the mangers, and there might be one or two in the hedge and some more in the pigsty. Be sure not to go near the sitty-hen in the coop."

Queenie pranced towards the door then stopped, and pouted.

"I'll not have time to win the prize for painting the most eggs if I've got to find the eggs as well!" she whined. "It's not fair!"

"Land's sake!" exclaimed Mrs Braithewaite. "There's no pleasing *some* people. Did ever you know such a child? Now then, Queenie, the sooner you're off the sooner you'll be back."

Robin followed Queenie out of the old dairy.

Marlene painted a trickle of green tears on an egg as brown as Earthy Mangold's face.

"It's not *fair*!" repeated Queenie when she and Robin were alone in the farmyard. "I ought to get two prizes—one for the prettiest faces and one for the most eggs. And I'm not going into the pigsty—that's a place for boys! It's for rough boys like you, Robin Elliot!"

Robin did not bother to answer. He had noticed the prints of pig-hooves outside the biggest sty, and he was away in a private world of his own.

Suppose, he thought. *Suppose a thief had stolen a three-legged pig——?*

His thoughts were interrupted by most peculiar noises coming from behind some brushwood and corrugated iron that was leaning slant-wise against the wall of one of the barns. The noises sounded like a mixture of sneezing, coughing, crowing, cawing and grunting.

Robin stood still to listen, and Queenie went on her whining way. The grunts were louder and more frequent than the other raucous noises, but they were not really pig-like.

P'raps, thought Robin, *P'raps a three-legged pig would talk like that. There were only three pig hoof-prints by the sty.*

He crept nearer to the brushwood as the grunts changed to spluttering. Could the noises be made by a three-legged pig with a very bad cold in its head? If so, and if Farmer Braithewaite had stolen it, then he (Robin) must find the right owner of a three-legged pig with a bad cold in its head. All the other pigs on the farm were pink and healthy. But why should Farmer Braithewaite want to steal an invalid pig? That was a mystery to be solved by a good detective.

The spluttering changed to cawing.

Pigs might fly! thought Robin, creeping closer.

There, sitting in a sort of tent of corrugated iron and wooden wall, sat Worzel Gummidge. Evidently he had been there for some time, and he must have been sitting very still, as was shown by a spiders' web spun between the rim of his old hat and the shoulder of his ragged jacket. (Robin felt proud of himself for noticing that.)

The scarecrow's broomstick legs were stuck straight out in front of him, and the toes of his bottle-straw boots

"Go away!" screeched Gummidge

pointed upwards. There was straw in his lap, too—straw and twigs and scraps of paper. In the middle of this muddle lay two large white eggs.

"Go away!" screeched Gummidge. "Go away, or you'll scare the hen that did ought to be comin' to lay. And" (as Robin stretched out a hand towards the eggs) "you can give over birds-nestin'."

"But Mrs Braithewaite sent me to collect eggs."

"Mrs Braithewaite allus lets the pot-eggs bide."

"Pot-eggs?" repeated Robin.

"Ooh aye! Pot-eggs is imitation eggs made out o' chiny. Mrs Braithewaite makes some o' the nests and puts pot-eggs in 'em. When a hen sees the pot-egg, she keeps on shoutin', 'If this nest were cosy enough for another lady, it'll be cosy enough for me!' Then she settles down an lays an egg hersel. Hens is easy taken in!"

"Did Mrs Braithewaite make this nest?" asked Robin.

Worzel Gummidge answered proudly, "I made it arter I'd took the pot-eggs from the mangers. I'm sick and tired o' robins makin' nests in my pockets and mice makin' nests in my boots. A good fierce hen'll keep 'em away: they can make their nests in other folk's pockets and other folk's boots. Now, leave me be to have a good sulk—me and the hen together. Hens is wunnerful sulkers when they're layin' and sittin'. They squats on the nest all huffed and puffed and sulky. Stands to reason it takes two to make a good sulk. Earthy never took to it proper."

Robin, suddenly remembering Earthy and his quest, said, "I promised Earthy I'd find you."

"When I wants findin' I'll find mesel."

For the second time that afternoon Robin heard himself explain, or trying to explain, to a scarecrow all about the methods of detectives.

From time to time Worzel Gummidge's eyes closed and his face looked more turnipy than ever. He showed every sign of falling into a deep sulk, but occasionally he stirred himself to argue.

"If I were a 'tecative I'd not need clues to know what's goin' on."

"If I were a 'tecative I'd not need lyin'-about-feathers to show me a bird were moultin'. I'd look at the bird goin' about in its skin and I'd *know* it were moultin.' Stands to reason!"

And—

"It's daft to look at human boot-marks seein' a humans changes their boots more often nor birds moults. Ooh Aye!"

And—

"What'd be the sense o' starin' at a sweep's finger-marks what'd be black one time, and white arter he'd licked 'em?"

While the arguments and explanations continued, a small, spangly bantam hen walked delicately round the corner, cackled boastingly that she was about to lay, settled down on the pot-eggs and ruffled her feathers.

Robin knew her quite well: she was the tame bird who spent so much of her time prating on the farmhouse doorstep.

"Very interferin' job bein' a 'tecative!" murmured Worzel Gummidge. "Now leave us be: we wants to sulk in private."

But before Robin could go away, furious screechings and cacklings sounded from behind the wooden wall that divided a barn from Gummidge's temporary home. An indignant hen was protesting. Queenie's shrill voice rose above the screeching.

"Don't peck me, you nasty thing, you!"

The little bantam hen blinked her golden eyes, and snuggled down more firmly on her nest.

Robin, peeping through a knot-hole in the wood, saw a dishevelled Buff Orpington fowl scutter past Queenie, fly to a wheelbarrow, stand on tip-claws, and stretch out its neck. Then it screeched its horror to the world.

Queenie was kneeling by a coop. One by one, she was taking eggs from a nest and mixing them with the others in her basket. She had propped up the door of the coop, and was working very hard.

Indeed, as the number of other eggs in the basket showed, she had been working hard ever since she had parted from Robin. This was not because she wanted to help the orphans, but because she hoped to win two prizes for herself.

The hen on the wheelbarrow continued to screech so dismally that Robin felt sorry for it.

"Shut up, or you'll have Mrs Braithewaite here!" shouted Queenie. "Shut up, silly!"

Robin put his mouth to the knot-hole, and yelled, "Put those eggs back! We were told not to disturb the sitting-hen. Put the eggs back before I make you!"

But before he could move, other voices were added to the clamour.

"It can't be a fox at this time of day!" cried Mrs Braithewaite.

Robin, once again peeping through the knot-hole, saw the farmer's wife, followed by Miss Dollit and Mrs Bloomsbury-Barton, rush into the barn.

"Something's being hurt," twittered Miss Dollit.

Queenie was caught—not red, but yellow-handed,

because she had broken an egg and the yolk was dripping between her fingers and on to her frock.

"You naughty little girl!" scolded Mrs Bloomsbury-Barton.

"That poor, poor hen!" squeaked Miss Dollit, going towards the bird, who lowered its beak and jabbed at her.

"Put those eggs back at once!" said Mrs Braithewaite. "I told you not to go near the sitty-hen. Put them back at once before she's too upset to sit on them."

There was silence for a moment, and then Queenie wailed, "I can't put them back. I don't know which they are. I've mixed them all up."

"Why did you mix them up?" demanded Mrs Braithewaite.

"So's you couldn't tell," whimpered Queenie, too dazed to be cunning.

"You're right there." Mrs Braithewaite's voice was very grim. "You're right there because most of our best layers are Buff Orpingtons."

"Such a quaint name!" put in Miss Dollit. "Such a very quaint name for a bird, and *so* unusual. Mrs Buff-Orpington would sound nearly as grand as Mrs Bloomsbury-Barton, wouldn't it? Mrs Buff-Orpington or, better still, Lady Buff-Orpington!"

If Mrs Bloomsbury-Barton's dress had been made of feathers, she would have ruffled it, as she said, "Don't be so absurd, Phoebe."

Mrs Braithewaite was peering down into the basket, and murmuring to herself. "There's a Rhode Island's egg that's a lot darker than the others. There's a White Leghorn's that's white. There's a pullet's and a bantam's: they're both smaller, but all the rest are Buff's."

On the other side of the wall, Robin was remembering that he was a detective. He had not lived in Scatterbrook for very long. He remembered other and older eggs, and turned excitedly to the scarecrow.

"The eggs Mum bought from the grocer had pictures of lions drawn on them. Do sitting-hens have eggs with lions on them?"

Very, very slowly Worzel Gummidge opened one eye.

"Don't be so daft! There's not a hen as'd demean hersel to draw picters on eggs. Mrs Braithewaite did ought to know as sitty-hens' eggs stays warm ten minutes or more arter the sitty-hen's come off o' the nest at feedin' time—tothers in the basket'll be cold by now."

The bantam hen winked, as though in agreement, but Robin did not stay long enough to see the wink.

"That's a fine clue!" he shouted, rushing out of the shelter and into the barn where Queenie was whimpering, "It's not fair! You told me to find a lot of eggs so's I could win prizes. Nothing's fair. Everyone's mean to me!"

"I've got a clue!" shouted Robin. "I've got a smashing clue!"

Mrs Bloomsbury-Barton spoke reprovingly, "We've no time to play silly games now, child."

"But it's not a game; it's a clue. The eggs under the sitty-hen will stay warm for ten minutes or more after she's left her nest!"

"Land's sake!" said Mrs Braithewaite. "Land's sake! The lad's right; I should have thought of that if I'd not been so flustered."

She stooped down to the basket again—"Here's a warm egg, here's another——"

Robin knelt down beside her.

Some of the eggs were warm against his knuckles. Some, at the tips of his exploring fingers, were cold as stones in winter. The warmth was magical and exciting.

Soon twelve eggs were lying in the nest of straw inside the coop.

Mrs Braithewaite straightened herself, shook chaff and straw from her apron, and walked gently towards the hen on the wheelbarrow.

"Chuckie, Chuckie, chuck-a-chuck," she crooned.

"K'ra-aa!" answered the hen, letting the feathers, that had been so ruffled by fear and fury, settle down into their rightful places.

Mrs Braithewaite put her hands (they were roughened by scouring churns and scrubbing floors, but gentle because of the orphan lambs she had cared for) carefully over the bird's wings, lifted her down, and settled her inside the coop.

"K'ra-aa!" said the hen, sinking down on the eggs.

"K'ra-aa! K'ra-aa!" she repeated.

Then, with her beak, she tucked an outlying egg under the soft feathers of her breast.

"Isn't nature wonderful!" exclaimed Miss Dollit. "Isn't Robin a clever little boy to have thought of such a good clue?"

"I can't understand how he did come to think of it before I did." Mrs Braithewaite spoke rather jealously. "It's not as though he was a proper country child."

Robin and his parents and little sister had only lived in Scatterbrook for a year. Before that they had lived in London.

"I wish he hadn't thought of it—that's all. He thought of it on purpose to stop me winning prizes!" Queenie flounced out of the barn.

"How *did* you think of it?" asked Mrs Bloomsbury-Barton.

"I just, sort of—well, I had a sort of hint from—from——" Robin hesitated because how could he explain that a scarecrow had helped him. "Well—a sort of, sort of friend of mine had a sort of—sort of clue!"

He was saved from more questions by a racket of noise from the other side of the wooden wall.

The little bantam hen, screeching wildly, hurried half-running, half-flying, past the doorway.

Louder and blood-curdling screeches and hissings sounded from Worzel Gummidge's hiding-place.

Queenie, looking as wild and dishevelled as the bantam, rushed into the barn.

"It keer-ed and hished at me!" she yelled. "It came at me, and pecked me. Look!"

She held out a wrist that showed a tiny pink mark, made so Robin guessed, by Gummidge's twiggy fingers.

"It hished and keer-ed at me. Look!"

"What?" asked Mrs Bloomsbury-Barton. "*What* did you say it did?"

"A great big giant of a hen—bigger than a turkey—and—and——"

"And, what, dear?" questioned Miss Dollit.

"The hen was wearing a HAT!"

"Nonsense!" Mrs Bloomsbury-Barton spoke severely. "Hens *never* wear hats. A great big girl like you should know that perfectly well. You must learn not to tell fibs, Queenie. Now pick up that basket, and come back to the dairy. We have wasted much too much time."

"It *did* have a hat on!" said Queenie sulkily, but not loudly enough for Mrs Bloomsbury-Barton to hear. "It ought to have its neck wrung. I'll send my Dad round to wring its neck. You see if I don't!"

The thought was so frightful that Robin ducked under Mrs Bloomsbury-Barton's elbow, pushed past Miss Dollit, and hurried to Gummidge's shelter.

"You heard what she said?" he gasped.

"Ooh aye!" The Scarecrow was standing up and shaking the remains of the bantam's nest from his shabby trousers. "Stands to reason!"

"If Queenie's Dad *does* wring your neck. I'll take his finger-prints from—from your——"

Robin hesitated because he could not see the Scarecrow's neck; the turnip head seemed to be fixed to the broomstick shoulders in some mysterious way.

"Wrung necks only matters to them as necks is bein' wrung. Asides, now I've started bein' a 'tecative, I'll take the finger-prints off of anyone as wrings me neck."

Suddenly, like a jack-in-the box, Worzel Gummidge jerked his head upwards and showed two inches of polished broomstick from behind his chin to the mystery of his shoulders.

"But you couldn't," argued Robin. "You couldn't take finger-prints *after* your neck had been wrung."

"You never know what you can do till you tries. Stands to reason! I'm goin' to be a 'tecative now. Bein' a 'tecative's easier nor what scarin' is. It were *me* as knew the sitty hen's eggs'd be warm."

3
General Weston's Goat

MISS DOLLIT was having a busy and rather difficult morning. She had offered to arrange the Easter Egg Hunt, but it was not easy to find suitable hiding-places for the eggs, because Mrs Braithewaite had declared that she would not allow the children from the Orphanage to "go trapesing and rampageing about the farmyard and the barns and chivying the poultry till they didn't know whether they were coming or going."

"Oh dear!" said Miss Dollit. "Oh dear! I'd had such a splendid idea, too. I'd meant to hide some of the Easter eggs by the new laid eggs in the hens' nests and the mangers."

"And," said Farmer Braithewaite, who was standing by, "I'll be glad if you'll keep out of my fields. I don't want gates left open by a pack of children, nor hedges broken down."

"Oh dear!" repeated Miss Dollit.

The conversation took place in the farmyard and was overheard by Robin and Marlene, who were hanging about in the hope of being asked to help in the preparation of tea for the visiting orphans. They looked forward to licking jam-spoons and scraping jelly from bowls and nibbling sweet and savoury crusts, cut off from sandwiches.

"Oh dear! That doesn't leave many hiding places, does it?"

Miss Dollit began to count on her fingers. "We can't hide eggs in the village street, because they'd be trodden on, and the orphans might be run over by cars. Perhaps the grocer would let us hide some eggs in his shop, and put some in the window."

"The grocer shuts on Saturday afternoon," reminded Mrs Bloomsbury-Barton.

"Oh dear! So does the Post Office! I don't think we ought to use Scatterbrook Station either, because the children might wander on to the line, and be run over."

"There aren't many trains," put in Robin, who knew all about the railway, because his Aunt Ruby lived at Station Cottage. It was almost his favourite place in Scatterbrook and was the home of Mildew Turmut, the Railway Scarecrow.

He wished he had not spoken, because Miss Dollit suddenly noticed him, and exclaimed, "You can help me—you and Marlene! We'll go up to the Downs, as that seems to be the only safe hiding-place"—(she glanced reproachfully at Mr and Mrs Braithewaite)—"and you kiddies can help me to hide the eggs. Then, this afternoon, you can go round with the orphans so that they don't get lost on the Downs. You can be *guides*!"

"Really, Phoebe!" said Mrs Bloomsbury-Barton. "Really, Phoebe, it won't be much of a hunt if the orphans are to be *guided* to the eggs!"

"I don't mean guided exactly. Perhaps, *shepherded* would be a better word. Robin and Marlene can give some little hints if some of the children seem discouraged or if a big one is finding more eggs than another."

"We can give them *clues*, you mean?" Robin spoke cheerfully, because he saw the chance of proving himself a good detective.

"Exactly!"

Just at that moment the most delicious scent of hot jelly drifted out of the farmhouse kitchen. Marlene sniffed wistfully, and asked, "Wouldn't we be more useful if we helped with the tea?"

"Do the thing that's nearest!" quoted Mrs Bloomsbury-Barton, though, really, the kitchen was nearer than the Downs.

Ten minutes later, Miss Dollit, Marlene and Robin, each carrying a basket, were hurrying up the lane that led to the top of the Downs.

At first, the egg-hiding was fun. Some of the painted eggs were half-buried in mole-hills, some in the shadows of sheep-hurdles and others in tussocks of coarse grass that had not attracted sheep.

"The cunning thing to do would be to hide the eggs among things that look like eggs," remarked Robin. "That would baffle these Orphanage 'tecs!"

"Yes," agreed Miss Dollit, "What a pity it isn't the right time of year for mushrooms!"

"If we were at the seaside we could hide them among stones," sighed Marlene. "I saw a film about sea-birds, and they laid their eggs among stones so nobody could tell which was which."

Robin collected some lumps of chalk from the entrance to a rabbit burrow, arranged them in a circle, and put an egg in the middle.

While he was doing this, Miss Dollit clapped her hands, as she always did when she was excited.

"I've a perfectly splendid idea! We'll go to the

golf-course and hide the eggs in the bunkers and other places. They'll look just like golf balls from a distance."

Now, the golf course at Scatterbrook was laid over part of the Downs. It was only a small nine-hole course on which a few elderly people took their morning exercise, lost their golf balls and their tempers, and found excellent appetites for lunch.

There was no club-house, and so the course was usually deserted on Saturday afternoons, when the elderly people, tired after exercise, pottered about in their gardens, rested, or read.

Because little spinneys, thick with brambles, were dotted about on the outskirts of the course, it was a favourite hunting place of the Scatterbrook children, who found many golf balls hidden in scratchy places or half-buried in the sand of the bunkers.

Marlene was particularly fond of it: she loved golf balls and liked to scrape off their white paint, and unwind the yards and yards and yards of thin elastic inside them. She knew the elastic would come in useful some day.

By the time, she, Miss Dollit and Robin, reached the course the golfers had gone home.

"Anyone could bury a body in one of those places," said Robin, pointing towards a bunker; "it would be as easy as anything, and his footprints wouldn't show in the sand. I wonder how 'tecs would find footprints in sand?"

"Robinson Crusoe did," argued Marlene.

"Then it must have been wet sand—wet, flat sand at the seaside just after the tide had gone out. Robinson Crusoe must have had an easy time being a 'tec."

"Man Friday wasn't a murderer." Marlene, too, had been reading the story of Robinson Crusoe, alone on his desert island until he found the footprints on the sand that showed where Man Friday had trodden.

"He may have been, AND a cannibal!"

"Children! Children!" interrupted Miss Dollit. "Can't you think of a prettier game? A lovely place like this reminds *me* of elves and gnomes and fairies—not of ugly people like murderers. But we shouldn't be playing games at all, should we? We ought to be hiding Easter eggs. Now, let's all go in different directions, and when we find a golf ball let's put an egg beside it. You'll remember that Marlene, dear, won't you?"

Marlene nodded rather gloomily—so gloomily that Miss Dollit added, "Perhaps, you and I had better go off together." She looked at her wrist-watch, and turned to Robin. "We can work for half an hour. At the end of that time, Marlene and I will cuckoo six times, and you'll know it's time to come home."

She skipped towards one of the greens, where little flags were flying, and Marlene followed her. Robin walked off in the direction of the nearest bunker—a hollow of sand with a half-circular mound of grassy turf surrounding it.

It's just the place, he thought, *it's just the place where a murderer might hide the man he'd murdered. Major Wazenby-Gunthorpe might've killed General Weston with a golf club and buried him in the sand, even if he doesn't look like a murderer. And General Weston might have killed one of the Rowstock brothers and dragged him up here in a coal-sack. It's the last place anyone'd think of looking for a Rowstock brother, because they don't play golf.*

He scrabbled about in the sand, found nothing but a cigarette end and a stub of pencil, hid two of the painted eggs, and hurried on to the next bunker, where he had no better luck.

Presently he noticed a flutter of white from the top of a bramble spray on the edge of a spinney, and dashed towards it.

It might be the murderer's hankie, he thought; *it may have initials on it, or bloodstains or finger-prints.*

The white stuff was a handkerchief, and a very clean large one. Also, it had embroidered initials on one corner.

Robin read them aloud. "W. G.! W. G.! Just as I thought—Wazenby-Gunthorpe."

"Beggin' your pardon, and if it's all the same to you, W.G. means Worzel Gummidge, and Mr Worzel Gummidge wouldn't demean hisel to use a cruel name like Wazenby-Gunthorpe."

Of course, Robin recognised the voice of Earthy Mangold. He was so used to finding the scarecrows in unexpected places that he was not at all surprised to see Gummidge's wife leaning up against a silver birch tree.

"But," he said, "but Worzel Gummidge doesn't use handkerchiefs like this."

Earthy looked sadly down at the banana-skin handkerchief sticking out from the pocket of her blue checked apron.

"If his name's wrote on it then it must be his." She gazed at the corner of the handkerchief that Robin held before her face. "Lot's of things have names wrote on 'em—Post Offices and railways and ploughs and the names *belongs* to the Post Offices and railways and ploughs."

Robin tried to explain that Major Wazenby-Gunthorpe and Scarecrow Worzel Gummidge had the same initials, but Earthy refused to understand him.

"My Worzel couldn't have nothin' the same as Major Wazenby-Gunthorpe," she said. "Major Wazenby-Gunthorpe's a nasty, bad, cruel man!"

"Do you mean he's a murderer?" Robin pocketed the handkerchief because now he felt that it really might become a clue.

"He's worse nor a murderer. I casn't hardly abide to tell you the wicked things he did this morning when he and that General Weston, that's so like a sheep, was hitting little white balls about and argufying which hit 'em harder."

Earthy shook some green tears from her eyes while Robin waited breathlessly.

"He said," she sobbed, "He said, 'You keep your eye on that ball, and don't you take your eye off that ball while you hits it!' "

"But——" began Robin, and then checked himself.

"Did ever you hear anything so cruel as to tell a genelman to put his eye on a ball and then hit it with a great bent bit o' iron. I casn't bear to think of it, and I couldn't abear to look while the poor, silly genelman took his eye out and put it on the ball. I covered me face with me aprin, but I heard the whack o' the club and I heard Major Wazenby-Gunthorpe shout, 'That's fine! You see what you can do when you don't take your eye off of the ball.' They was argufyin' and quarrellin' when they went away. You couldn't blame General Weston for argufyin' and quarellin' arter he'd hit his poor eye like that, and maybe lost it for ever."

If Earthy had not sobbed so loudly, Robin might have heard six piercing "cuckoo" cries from Miss Dollit, who had discovered that her watch had stopped. Even if he had heard, perhaps he would not have hurried down to the village, because Earthy stopped sobbing as suddenly as she had begun, and spoke quite fiercely:

"Someone did ought to tell the perlice about Major

Wazenby-Gunthorpe havin' stole General Weston's goat. General Weston needs a deal o' comfortin' seein' he'll not be able to look for it so easy with only one eye. Very cunnin' Major Wazenby-Gunthorpe were to tell General Weston to put his eye on the ball and hit it. He must a done it o' purpose so's the General couldn't find his goat."

The day brightened for Robin. Now was the chance to prove himself a real detective. He asked eagerly. "Are you sure Major Wazenby-Gunthorpe stole a goat? How do you know?"

"General Weston said so, and Major Wazenby-Gunthorpe didn't say he'd not. Seems it weren't the first time neither, acos General Weston said he'd do it once too often. I heard him say so quite plain. It were in the quarrel afore the last quarrel arter Major Wazenby-Gunthorpe had stole a ball as General Weston said were his."

"Coo!" breathed Robin and, as from across the fairway came the sound of bleating, he shouted "There's the goat!"

Earthy Mangold addressed a spider who was weaving a beautiful web between two sprays of a bramble bush.

" 'You'll get my goat once too often!' That's what General Weston said."

Robin, of course, did not hear her. Major Wazenby-Gunthorpe's handkerchief flapped from his pocket as he ran in the direction of the bleating.

It was the habit of sheep to graze the Scatterbrook golf links, and they were useful because they kept the grass on the greens cropped closely. Six or seven of them raised their mild faces as Robin reached one of the greens, but there was not a goat among them.

There are lots more sheep I expect, he thought, *I wonder if Major Wazenby-Gunthorpe'd hide a stolen goat among sheep—that would be the clever thing to do because people would hear it bleating and think it was sheep like I'd have done if I hadn't been a 'tec. I don't know if Major Wazenby-Gunthorpe's clever or not. If he's not clever he'll have hidden it at home and then someone's sure to hear it bleating and he'll be copped. Wish I knew where to look first.*

As he puzzled over his problems, Robin kicked at the turf on the green in a way that would have enraged both Major Wazenby-Gunthorpe and General Weston.

A little flag was fluttering beside a hole in the turf. It was a neat round hole and in it were two of the Easter eggs that Robin had painted the day before.

I s'pose Marlene hid them there—or Miss Dollit, he thought. *I suppose I ought to hide the rest of my eggs before we go home.*

He glanced into his basket, and was surprised to see only three eggs where at least a dozen had been before.

"I'd better hide these," he said to one of the sheep, but before he could think of a hiding-place he noticed a tag of wool clinging to the top of the tiny iron flagstaff, and picked it up.

The wool was damp still from the morning dew. Robin thought it would make a false moustache—*good disguise for a 'tec*, and pressed it to his upper lip.

A faint tang of sheep reached his nose. He sniffed and thought and sniffed again.

Goats smell strong, he thought. *Marlene's mother sold their billy-goat that smelled so strong. My hands smelled like billy-o after I stroked the goat. Sheep don't smell much*, he sniffed again, *not much, only like the stuff Dad oils his garden boots with. There's lots of tufts of sheep wool caught on bushes and barbed wire and hurdles. If I find some goaty tufts I can follow the trail and find General Weston's goat.*

He turned and shouted to the astonished sheep—"That's a smashing clue!"

For half an hour or so, he wandered round the outskirts of the links, diving among the brambles and last year's bracken snatching shreds and tags of wool, sniffing them, and being disappointed because there was no tang of goat on any of them.

Presently, he began to feel hungry, was surprised not to have heard Miss Dollit's cuckooing, and decided she must have forgotten him. Then he sat down to rest and think. There was no doubt that being a detective was hard and hungry work.

A 'tec must eat, he thought. *It's important for a 'tec to eat to have strength enough to find General Weston's goat. I deserve an egg or two for working so hard.*

It happened that the eggs in the basket were the ones that had been painted by Queenie. Robin rather enjoyed cracking the silly, painted face against a branch, but he did not enjoy the taste of the egg. Perhaps this was because his feeling of guiltiness did not make up for the loss of salt.

He choked down two more eggs, yawned, stretched himself out and went to sleep, his cheek against damp twigs.

He dreamed a curious, muddled dream in which he and a goat, each dressed in policeman's uniform, were arresting Major Wazenby-Gunthorpe for stealing Mrs Bloomsbury-Barton's best hat. The goat wore a wrist-watch just above its right fore hoof, and its long beard was egg-stained. "Anything you say," said the goat, "anything you say will be taken down and may be used in evidence against you. Do you wish to consult your solicitor?" Major Wazenby-Gunthorpe replied that he wished to consult Mr Worzel

Gummidge. Then the dream changed unexpectedly in the strange manner of dreams, and Robin was being pursued by a crowd of children from the Holiday Home. "We're having a boy hunt!" they shouted. "Robin's the boy who stole our eggs!"

Every child had pink cheeks and golden hair and blue eyes and egg-shaped faces; instead of fingers, they had tufts of sheep's wool. Their finger-nails were bramble thorns.

Robin (still in his dream, of course) tried to run faster and faster, but he felt as though he were running in deep sand that came above his knees and prevented his joints from working properly.

"We must, we must, we must," bleated the children as their voices came nearer and nearer, "we must, we must catch Robin, kill him, eat him, we must, we must, we MUST!"

Then, as happens in the most important part of a dream when things are becoming too important or wonderful or exciting or frightening, Robin awakened with a jerk.

For a moment he did not know where he was. He only knew that he was safe—that an empty and quite ordinary basket was lying beside him, and that something hard was pressing into his cheek.

He sat up, and brushed a knobbly twig from his cheek. As a matter of fact, he did not know (quite) where he was, because he had not noticed before he ate the eggs, slept and dreamed, that he was in a copse quite near to the flag whose top had been decorated by a tag of wool.

Now, from his resting-place, he heard the sound of heavy breathing, and peeped through the bracken. Major Wazenby-Gunthorpe was taking very careful aim at a golf ball that was lying only about eight inches from the hole below the flag. He had come up to practise his putting because he was determined to beat General Weston.

I bet, thought Robin, *I bet he's only bluffing. He's just pretending to play golf, but he's come to find that goat. If I wait and follow him—sleuth him—I'll see where he's hidden the goat.*

Major Wazenby-Gunthorpe tapped the ball just a little too hard. It rolled towards the hole, balanced half in, half out of it, and rolled on.

"Extraordinary thing!" said Major Wazenby-Gunthorpe to himself. "Most extraordinary thing! It's against all the laws of nature!"

He strode forward, knelt down and peered into the hole. Then he pulled out two eggs.

"Queer place for hens to lay!" he muttered. "Queer eggs too!"

The face of the policeman, painted by Robin, glared up at him.

Now, he was not a particularly bad-tempered man, but he had had an unlucky day. First he had quarrelled with his friend, General Weston, who could be very irritating indeed. Then he had eaten a very horrid lunch—watery stew with underdone potatoes and soggy cabbage, followed by a much too suetty pudding. Then he had a second long and tiring walk to the golf-course. Now, so he thought, someone had played a practical joke on him. He flung the eggs down, stamped on one and kicked the other.

Neither he nor Robin had noticed that a strange small boy had crept up to the edge of the green. He was holding a cap full of eggs (they were the ones spilled from Robin's basket when he had rushed across the fairway a long time ago) and he was looking proud and happy.

"Coo!" exclaimed the little boy.

"Don't hit him!" yelled Robin, as he seized Major Wazenby-Gunthorpe's putter

Major Wazenby-Gunthorpe swung round, saw him, saw the eggs and spluttered: "You—you, so it's you! What do you mean by trespassin' on the links and layin'—hidin' your beastly eggs all over the place?"

The skinny little boy dropped his cap, and turned to run away.

Shouting, "Come here, boy!" Major Wazenby-Gunthorpe swung his putter wildly.

It was then that Robin did the bravest deed of his life because the little boy was so very little and Major Wazenby-Gunthorp looked so large and fierce.

"Don't hit him!" yelled Robin, and, dashing through the brambles, he seized Major Wazenby-Gunthorpe's putter.

The small boy rushed away like a scared rabbit.

Robin clung to the head of the putter, and gasped, "If you hit him, I'll tell everyone you stole General Weston's goat!"

"What the——? Who the——?" puffed Major Wazenby-Gunthorpe, also clinging to the putter. "Of course I wasn't going to hit him. Why are the links stiff with children? Seen you before somewhere, haven't I?"

"Yes, sir." Robin was not feeling at all brave now. If he had stopped to think, he would not have left his hiding-place.

"Who are you?"

"Robin Elliot." He was only little Robin Elliot now, *quite* little Robin Elliot who lived with his parents and baby sister. He was not likely to turn into Chief Inspector Elliot of Scotland Yard. His only consolation was that the smaller boy was safe.

"Well, don't come footlin' round the links again. Stick to your marbles in the playground."

Robin felt smaller than ever.

"You can take your pal's cap with you, and you can take those eggs, too. Fond of eggs, eh?"

"Not—not very, sir."

Robin did not feel in the very least fond of eggs as he retrieved half a dozen of them and stuffed them into the red flannel cap.

"Well, don't play fool tricks with them, then."

It was no use trying to explain; explanations would have taken too long, and he was in a hurry to go.

"Be off with you now. No; wait a bit! What did you say about a goat and General Weston?"

Robin hesitated. Major Wazenby-Gunthorpe did not look like a goat-stealer, but then did goat-stealers look like goat-stealers any more than murderers looked like murderers?

"I—you—"

"Out with it, boy!"

"General Weston's goat—" gulped Robin.

"General Weston's goat. He hasn't got a goat. Don't talk nonsense, boy. He hasn't got a goat, has he?"

"N—not now!" stammered Robin.

"What do you mean?"

"Not now that you've—that you've GOT it! He said you had."

Major Wazenby-Gunthorpe glared and then smiled and then laughed. He looked even less like a goat-stealer while he was laughing.

"You'd better tell me all about it, boy!" he said.

Robin tried to tell him—not everything, of course, because it would have been too difficult to have explained about Earthy Mangold—but he said that he was trying to be a detective and that a friend had told him that General

Weston had said that Major Wazenby-Gunthorpe had stolen (Robin used the word "pinched" because he thought it sounded more polite than "stolen") his goat, and that he would do it once too often.

At the end, his listener laughed more loudly than ever.

"To get a person's goat means to make him lose his temper: it's just an expression. Your friend must be a bit stupid."

Earthy Mangold isn't quite so clever as Worzel Gummidge, thought Robin.

"General Weston and I are always 'getting each other's goats'," added Major Wazenby-Gunthorpe, "but we're very good friends. Now cut along after your pal. Wait a bit. Here's a sort of medal for standing up to me. Now cut along."

Robin "cut".

As he hurried across the fairway, and along the little lane that led to the village he decided that, though his day's detecting had ended rather flatly, he was glad that Major Wazenby-Gunthorpe was not a goat-stealer: he would not have been happy in prison, and General Weston would have missed him.

He wondered if the little boy had found his way down to Scatterbrook. By now he was feeling hungry enough to eat the eggs in the red cap, but he was feeling much too thirsty. Presently he stumbled against a stone. The eggs rolled out of the cap, and he left them lying in a cluster by a clump of grass.

He thought of orange squash, and ginger-pop and raspberryade and Coca-Cola.

"I'll buy the lot when I get to the Post Office," he told himself as he jogged down the lane. "I'll buy a bottle of each and I'll start with ginger-pop. I can *afford* to buy the lot now!" For in his pocket was the half-crown given by Major Wazenby-Gunthorpe, "as a sort of medal for standing up to me."

Then he remembered it was Saturday and that the Post Office was shut.

"Oh well," said Robin to himself. "I'll keep the half-crown as a medal. When I'm a proper 'tec I'll wear it to remind me of today."

But today was not over. When Robin reached the village green, he saw a coach. Clustered beside it were about twenty strange children, some Scatterbrook boys and girls, Mrs Bloomsbury-Barton, Miss Dollit and a grey-haired, rosy-faced woman, who was reading names from a list—"Katie Stubbs, Maurice Gilbey, Shirley Brooks, Frances Meadows, Albert King, Barbara Street, Wallace James, Mabel Wright, Ann Stubbington."

As their names were read out, the children raised their hands. Robin noticed that most of the hands were clutching painted eggs.

The reading continued—"Marjorie Newborn, Alec Brown, Phillip Kendall, Grace Adams, Walter Price, Phyllis Lacey, Martin Price——"

There was a pause: all the hands remained down.

"Martin Price? MARTIN PRICE?"

"Oh dear!" twittered Miss Dollit. "I hope the child isn't lost."

Miss Grace (she was the rosy-cheeked woman who had brought the children from the Orphanage) looked very worried as she asked, "Has anyone seen Martin Price?"

Several hands shot up, and several children spoke at once, saying they had seen Martin just after they arrived in Scatterbrook, but not since.

Suddenly, a small girl pointed to Marlene. "He was with HER," she announced. "He and some of the rest of us were with her."

At once all the grown-ups questioned Marlene.

"Was Martin Price with you? Where did you see Martin Price? When did you see him last? Did he seem unhappy? Did he look lost?"

"I didn't know his name." Marlene answered rather sulkily, "I don't know any of their names."

Miss Dollit asked the only sensible questions. "Do you think he went up to the golf-course? Did you send him there to look for Easter eggs?"

"I sort of hinted, like you told me to, I said there might be eggs up there. I said it to some of them who were fed up with not finding eggs, and——"

Mrs Bloomsbury-Barton interrupted, "Phoebe! Surely you didn't hide eggs on the links—so very far away?"

"I'm afraid I did. I wanted to make the hunt more exciting for the children. Oh dear! I shall never forgive myself if anything has happened to the poor little boy."

"I should hope not!" said Mrs. Bloomsbury-Barton. "Now the tea which is ready at the farm must be delayed because a small boy is lost."

"One moment, please!" Miss Grace stepped forward, and spoke loudly. "Did anyone see Martin Price on the golf-links? Did anyone see a little boy on the links?"

There was a long long pause, and the question was repeated—"Did anyone—this is most important—see a boy on the links?"

Robin, who had been looking enviously at an iced lolly (to him the most important thing in the world, just at that moment) being waved and sucked alternately by a child at his side, answered.

"Yes!"

Now it was his turn for questioning.

"Where, *exactly*, did you see him? Was he very small—this from Miss Grace—much smaller than you are, and with rather sticking-out teeth?" Robin nodded in answer to the last question.

"What was he doing?"

"He was running away!"

"Why? Where? Did he tell you his name? Was he frightened by anything? Where was he running *to*?"

Robin, feeling that hens had been beating their wings round his head, answered the last question simply and truthfully. "He was just running away."

"But how queer!" put in Miss Dollit. "Why should he want to run away? Has anyone bullied him? What a very odd kiddy to want to *run away* from a lovely Easter egg hunt and a wonderful tea!" She turned to Robin, "Was he running away from anything or anyone?"

The questions were too complicated to answer. Explanations would have meant telling about Earthy Mangold and the goat that wasn't a real goat and Major Wazenby-Gunthorpe. Robin sighed heavily, and replied, "I saw him running away and then I didn't see him any more. He was just running away."

"But WHY?"

Mrs Bloomsbury-Barton had asked the last question, but Robin was saved from answering by the brisk voice of Miss Grace. "Martin Price *is* rather an odd little boy. He is a child who likes to be alone. His great interest is 'train-spotting'—that's what he calls it. Is there a railway station here?"

Norma, sister of Jim, the railway porter, spoke up importantly: "The train should be in about now!"

"Then there's no time to lose!" exclaimed Mrs Bloomsbury-Barton. "There's no time to lose if the boy really was running away or train-*stopping*. Follow me!"

Pushing and chattering, some of them anxious and others excited at the thought of an accident, the visiting children and the boys and girls of Scatterbrook, followed the grown-up people towards the little railway station.

Robin was too thirsty to think of anything but water. In a paddock behind the green there was a cattle trough, and above the trough there was a pipe, and a tap.

He ran across the green, scrambled over a gate and hurried towards the trough. Lying full length in it, his head and the tips of his bottle-straw boots just showing above the water, was Worzel Gummidge.

"Arternoon!" said the scarecrow pleasantly, "I'm havin' a washin'-day."

Robin turned on the tap, put his mouth to the stream of water, sucked, spluttered, felt better and shook drops from his hair. Then he drank again, and yet again.

"You can share with me if you've the fancy," said Gummidge, "I'm not partickler."

As he turned off the tap, Robin looked down into the muddy water.

"I don't want a bath."

"I didn't ask you to have a bath. I were invitin' you to a drink. Stands to reason water in the trough's stronger and tastier arter my clothes has been lying in it."

Now, Robin was not a particular boy—not particularly particular. He had no objection to toffee that had collected pocket-fluff, or to lollies that had been dropped on pavements or even to turnabout licks of ice-cream, but he answered: "I don't drink bath-water!" Fearing he had been impolite, he added, "I don't even drink my own bath-water: I don't like the taste of soap."

"It's wunnerful what humans does like the taste of—dead fishes and cows and pigs and milk that comes out o' cows and eggs that comes out o' hens."

"Well, I don't like the taste of dirt that comes out of clothes."

"There's bits o' dirt does come out o' clothes; more's the pity." Gummidge looked gloomily at the flecks of mud, bits of straw and other rubbish floating round him in the water. "If I were dirty enough I'd not need a washin'-day. Stands to reason, I'd be heavy enough without."

"Heavy enough?" repeated Robin.

"Ooh aye! Humans, bein' daft, has washin'-days to make theirsels and their clothes lighter acos dirt weighs heavy. Scarecrows, *not* bein' daft, has washin'-days to make 'emsels heavy—trouble is dirt comes off in water. If we'd enough dirt on us we'd not need washin'-days."

"We wash to be clean," argued Robin.

"What's the sense o' *clean*? Clean don't stick like mud. I'm havin' a washin' day acos the wind's gettin' up and I'm goin' back to scarin'. If you was a scarecrow, you'd know the obstinacy o' tryin' to stand up in a gale—your rags blowin' round like hen feathers. When I've had a good soak, I can stand up steady in any gale. Soggy clothes don't flap and soggy clothes is heavy. Stands to reason."

The scarecrow raised his dripping arms. "Give us a pull-out afore me legs starts warpin'."

Robin tugged and hauled, but Gummidge was as unhelpful as a wooden doll when it is being dressed. Once or twice, he flopped back into the water with such a splash that the boy's shirt and shorts became soused with muddy wetness. He did not like to complain for fear of being despised for having "daft" ideas about washing-day.

At last, when the two were sitting side by side on the edge of the trough, Worzel Gummidge asked, "Have you seen Earthy layin' about anywheres?"

Robin described some of the events of the morning, and ended up by asking, "Did you see a boy running away?"

"I seed lots o' boys runnin' all ways. Scatterbrook's full o' them—girls, too."

"This one's name is Martin Price."

"He can call hisel what he likes—it don't make no differ. You calls yoursel Robin arter a bird, but you don't go on like a bird. Martin's a bird name, but boys don't make fiddlin' mud nests under house-roofs."

"I never said they did!" snapped Robin, who was confused by argument, and irritable through hunger now that he had quenched his thirst.

"Nor I didn't neither—I said as they didn't!"

"Anyway"—Robin pulled the crumpled cap from his pocket—"anyway, I've got his cap, and"—he peeped inside the rather grubby lining—"and his name's inked inside it—MARTIN PRICE. So there!"

"So where?" asked Worzel Gummidge maddeningly. "What's the sense o' findin' a cap when you're lookin' for a boy?"

"Because, if you find a thing that belongs to a person, it can tell you where the person's been."

"Ask the cap then, and don't come botherin' me! Stands to reason it's daft to find a thing when you're lookin' for a person, and it's more daft to think you know where he is acos you know where he's been. Stands to reason!"

"But I don't know where he is."

"If I'd lost a spadger, supposin' I had a spadger and

supposin' I were daft enough to want it, I'd not demean mesel to go flutteratin' round arter it and pickin' up its moulted feathers. I'd go to Mrs Braithewaite's yard at hen-feedin' time. Spadgers allus goes to food same as boys does. Stands to reason."

The word *food* made Robin remember his hunger, the name Braithewaite reminded him of the glorious tea waiting for the orphans in the farmhouse kitchen.

"A 'tec"—he began and had meant to add: "A 'tec must eat!"

Worzel Gummidge interrupted—"I'm the best 'tecative hereabouts!"

Martin Price may have found the tea, thought Robin as he turned and ran away. *He may like eating better than train-spotting. I like it better. Besides——*

Martin Price *had* found the tea. Evidently he *did* like eating better than he liked train-spotting, as Robin discovered when he opened the door that led into the kitchen.

The other boy was sitting at one end of a laden trestle-table, and his plate was laden, too. It was clear that he had been taught not to speak with his mouth full, because he did not say a word as Robin joined him. He only rubbed a fruit-juicy-flaky-pastry moustache from his upper lip before beginning to grow a Coca-Cola-ham-sandwichy moustache in its place.

Robin ate four sausage rolls, three ham sandwiches and a dollop of raspberry jelly, and drank two glasses of lemonade before he spoke.

"Thought I'd find you here. You *are* Martin Price, aren't you?"

The skinny little boy nodded, and transferred a raspberry-jelly-biscuit-crumby moustache from his mouth to the peak of the cap that Robin held out to him.

Miss Dollit's agitated voice, asking Mrs Braithewaite if she might telephone to the police, sounded in the passage.

"We'd better scram!" said Robin, and Martin Price followed him out of the kitchen and into the passage where the telephone stood.

"I've found him!" yelled Robin as Miss Dollit's trembling hand moved towards the receiver.

"Where? . . . Oh what a relief! . . . Where had he been? . . . How very fortunate!" Miss Dollit spoke gaspingly, and then turned to Martin Price: "Are you all right, dear? Not hurt?"

The skinny little boy shook his head while scrubbing his mouth on the cap peak.

"Oh NOT on your cap, dear. You'll spoil it. Haven't you got a hankie?"

Again Martin Price shook his head.

"I haven't got one either. Robin? Yes, you have." Miss Dollis tugged at a flutter of white dangling from the boy's pocket. "What a grand hankie!"

It was Robin's turn to shake his head. "He can't have that—it's Major Wazenby-Gunthorpe's. I found it when I was looking for——"

"And finding!" broke in Miss Dollit. "You are a splendid *finder*—quite a little detective!"

Robin grinned, but the grin faded as he remembered Worzel Gummidge's boast—"I'm the best 'tecative hereabouts!"

Later, when he was finishing his second tea, he thought: *Next time I'll finish my sleuthing by myself, and I'll be the best 'tec.*

4
Hidden Treasure

NOBODY KNEW how old the story was or why it had been revived so suddenly, but the whole of Scatterbrook was agog with legend and gossip. Men talked of it in the *Red Lion*, women made guesses over their gates, and the children chattered like starlings.

The rumour was that there was "treasure at Turkeys," and that the treasure had lain hidden for years and years and years.

"Turkeys" was owned by old Mrs Corderoy. It was a Tudor cottage, beamed and thatched and colour-washed; and it stood a little way back from the Scatterbrook village street. There was a tiny, flower-dotted garden in front with a brick path leading to the front door. At the back there was a big vegetable patch, separated from the Downs by a wobbling track.

The only signs of vegetables were tough stumps, from which brussels sprouts had sprouted about a year ago, the frondy leaves of carrots, horse-radish, a few determined artichokes and a bush of sage. Had it not been for these, the patch could have been described as a "weed garden." Thistles and nettles, chickweed and groundsel ramped: bindweed tried to choke the lot.

Mrs Corderoy was not a good gardener. She was fond of saying, "It's my bad leg that stops me from having green fingers, but you should have seen the begonias on my old gran's window-ledge."

There were lots of Corderoys in Scatterbrook—nephews and nieces and other relations of the owner of "Turkeys." It was said that at the time of William the Conqueror the name had been *Cœur de Roi* (heart of the King) and that one of the family had sailed from Normandy with the King.

"P'raps the treasure's French money—gold Napoleons and things," said Robin vaguely, after he had heard the story.

"Don't be silly. Napoleon came years and years after William the Conqueror." Marlene spoke in a showing-off voice.

"There might be William the Conqueror money AND Napoleons. French relations may have come to stay at 'Turkeys' years and years after William the Conqueror, and left their money there."

Robin tugged up a root of groundsel and flung it down by one of Upsidaisy's three milking-stool legs. He and Marlene were working on one of the school allotments, where "the eddicated Scarecrow," as Upsidaisy called herself, worked.

It was one of the rules of Scatterbrook School that each pupil should do a little gardening on each fine day of the holidays. It was not a popular plan.

Upsidaisy was wearing her usual clothes—a green velveteen coat, a sailor hat, stuffed woollen gloves and socks of three different colours.

"It doesn't do to grumble!" chirruped Upsidaisy. "No, it doesn't do to grumble, but spadgers likes groundsel and if you pulls it all up I'll not be able to scare the spadgers as doesn't come to peck the groundsel as isn't there."

"Groundsel comes up easier than grass and stuff," said Robin. "I hate weeding. I wouldn't mind if there was a chance of finding buried treasure."

He leaned on his fork and stared down at the ground, because an idea had come into his mind.

If Mrs Corderoy would let me dig in her garden, I might find the treasure. Bet you anything I would, because now I'm a 'tec I know how to look for clues. If my spade hit something that rang, I'd know there was an iron chest underneath and I wouldn't just go on digging across, I'd dig deep and pull up the box. They always buried treasure in iron boxes. P'raps the box would be locked. Then I'd have to ask the blacksmith to open it or, wait a bit—Marlene's got lots of keys.

"Hi! Marlene! Will you lend me your keys?"

Marlene had stopped gardening. As usual, she was "collecting". She had made a little heap of round white pebbles and was polishing another on the edge of her cardigan.

"What for?"

"To open an old iron box."

"Where is it?"

"Dunno yet—not exactly, but I'll find it."

"That old treasure of Mrs Corderoy's? If it was there, it would have been dug up years ago. 'Sides, she wouldn't let you keep it."

"Treasure trove belongs to the Crown!" piped Upsidaisy. "I know that acos o' bein' eddicated and listnin' to histry under the school winders. It doesn't do to grumble, but I wishes the holidays was over so's I could go on with my eddication."

"But finding's keeping," argued Robin. "I'd give some to Mrs Corderoy if she wanted it."

"What crown d'you mean?" asked Marlene.

"Any crown what's lying about—the Queen's crown if she'd happened to leave it lyin' about in Mrs Corderoy's garden. You wouldn't think a crown'd want a lot o' treasure, seein' it's so heavy to start with. Queen Victoria's crown were too heavy for her little neck—that's histry, too. You'd think they'd make queens with thick strong necks seein' they has to wear heavy great crowns, but they don't, so that's all there is about it."

Robin thought hard, and then said, "Not likely the Queen would leave her crown lying about in Mrs Corderoy's garden!"

"Upsidaisy means the treasure would belong to the Queen. Crown's short for Queen or King." Marlene counted on her fingers, "No, it's not—it's long—doesn't matter. Anyway, my Dad says Mrs Corderoy once found an Elizabethan sixpence in her garden. He says that's how the treasure story started."

"Coo!" exclaimed Robin, and his mind began to work very quickly—so quickly that Upsidaisy's next rambling information was only a slight interruption:

"Queen Elizabeth the First slept in lots o' differ places—she were like a gipsy, 'cept she liked sleepin' in beds, and gipsies likes sleepin' loose. She slept in hundreds o' differ beds—that's in histry, too. Maybe she couldn't find a bed to suit her. 'Uneasy lies the head that wears a crown.' *That's* an eddicated sayin' in histry. Maybe she slept in Scatterbrook and couldn't settle comfortable and threw her crown out o' the winder and it rolled in Mrs Corderoy's garden."

Robin flung down his fork, and raced away too soon to

hear the rest of Upsidaisy's lecture: "It's in histry that we've all started bein' Elizabethans all over again. They say in eddication as 'Histry allus repeats itsel'."

He neither heard the words nor Marlene's footsteps as she pounded after him. He did not notice the gossiping starlings on the cottage roofs; his thoughts were much too busy.

An Elizabethan sixpence is a smashing clue. Where there was one there must be lots. Nobody would bury just one sixpence—not unless he was very poor. Wonder what part of the garden Mrs Corderoy found it in. It might have tipped out of the iron box when it was being buried, so the box should be near. I've not had much luck being a 'tec yet, but now I'll show 'em. I don't want any of the other children. Good 'tecs won't have lots of people tramping all over the place and treading on clues. Even a few Elizabethan sixpences must be worth a lot. My dad has a gold sovereign that's worth nearly four pounds, and it's not even in history. I've got to look at that sixpence to see what the rest'll look like.

Panting from loss of breath and excitement he arrived at Mrs Corderoy's front gate, flung it open, ran up the path and knocked impatiently at the door.

Before it could be opened, Marlene had joined him.

"What do you want?" asked Robin.

"Just to come with you," answered Marlene.

After all, she was his greatest friend and it would be rather mean not to let her join in the excitement.

"O.K.," said Robin. "But you mustn't trample about."

The door opened and Mrs Corderoy faced them. She was a rather witch-like old woman with big, dark, bristly eyebrows and glittering eyes and a hooky nose. She hobbled on a stick, but she looked fierce enough to have come over *herself* with William the Conqueror.

"What do you want?" asked Mrs Corderoy.

"Please," said Robin, "please to look at the sixpence."

"The very idea!" snapped Mrs Corderoy, who was slightly deaf. "I've plenty to do with my own sixpences—let alone give them to you. I don't know what children are coming to. Give you sixpence, indeed."

The door was beginning to shut, and Robin shouted loudly and desperately, "I only want to *look*. If we find any more, we'll give some of them to you."

Mrs Corderoy smiled toothlessly. "You want to give me sixpence? It's very kind I'm sure, but I wouldn't want to rob you."

"*No!*" shouted Robin.

"No, I should think I wouldn't rob you, but thank you all the same."

A gust of spring wind came to the rescue: it fluttered Mrs Corderoy's scarf and sent straw from the thatch whirling on to the doorstep.

"Come in!" she said. "I can't stand out in this draught all morning: it's enough to cut one in half. Come in and tell me what you want."

The children followed her into the cottage.

"I was just making myself a cup of tea," said Mrs Corderoy, taking a tea-pot from the mantelshelf. "No; not that one. Dunno what I'm thinking of!"

As she thumped the teapot down again, a rattling and clinking came from its inside. If Robin had been a terrier, his ears would have pricked up.

Mrs Corderoy took another teapot from the shelf, tipped tea into it and poured boiling water from a kettle standing on a smoky oil stove.

"I'll be glad to get out of this place and no mistake. Soon as I can sell it, I'll be joining my niece in one of the new Council houses—electricity and electric boiler—all modern and none of this smoke and jackdaws' nests in the chimleys. I'd go tomorrow, but a place goes to pieces once it's been standing empty for any time. It needs doing up as 'tis—so does the garden need digging over."

A terrier's ears would have pricked again.

Mrs Corderoy opened a tin and dumped some very rocky rock buns in front of the children. They tasted as smoky as the room looked.

Between dry mouthfuls, Robin spoke hopefully: "We could dig the garden for you: we could sweep the chimney." (He had remembered that treasure is found, sometimes, in old chimneys.) "We'd dig deep."

"So that's it, is it?" Mrs Corderoy spooned sooty sugar into her cup. "You'll be Bob-a-job ones. I had some of them once, pretending to be Boy Scouts, which they weren't, and smearing the windows with greasy rags and then having the sauce to charge a shilling apiece. I gave one to the lot of 'em, and grudged that. What was it *you* said about sixpence?"

Mrs Corderoy's mind seemed to dart about as quickly as a rabbiting dog, but her last question gave Robin his chance, and he said, "We only want to look at that old sixpence—the Elizabeth one—that you dug up in your garden."

"So's we'll know what they look like if we find any more," put in Marlene.

"Oh *that*!" Mrs Corderoy hobbled over to the mantelshelf and took down the teapot that had rattled. "Well, there's no harm in looking, I don't suppose."

She lifted the lid and then cleared a space on the

There lay a quite unexciting-looking coin

muddled table. Robin expected to see gold and silver pouring out, and caught his breath as Mrs Corderoy turned the teapot upside down.

The treasure was disappointing: ordinary pennies, halfpennies, sixpences and threepenny bits came clinking down and a shower of dust rose up.

"I keep this handy for paying the baker and the fish," muttered Mrs Corderoy. "Funny about that old sixpence!"

She shook the teapot again and something else fell out of it. The something was wrapped in a scrap of yellowed newspaper. Mrs Corderoy fumbled for what seemed as long as an arithmetic lesson.

"My fingers are all thumbs today," she grumbled and then held out her hand. There on her furrowed palm lay a quite unexciting-looking coin. It was so thin that it reminded the children of the money they had laid on the railway lines in the hope of turning sixpences into shillings. The coin was so flattened that the face of Queen Elizabeth the First looked almost rubbed out.

"May I feel it?" asked Marlene.

The coin was as light as it looked and its clipped edges were quite sharp. Robin noticed this as he took it from Marlene and held it up to the light.

"It's not very shiny, is it?" he said.

"I've always meant to give it a rub-up," sighed Mrs Corderoy, "but what with having so much to do and my leg being so bad I've never got round to it."

Robin rubbed the coin on his shorts until it began to look more like treasure.

"That'll do, now," said Mrs Corderoy. "You don't want to rub it away!"

When the sixpence had been re-wrapped and put back

in the teapot at the bottom of the other coins, the children asked their questions and listened to the rambling answers.

Mrs Corderoy had found the sixpence two or three years ago. No, she had not dug it up; it was not in an iron box nor in the chimney. She had seen it sticking up in the middle of a mole-hill in the back garden.

"Where *exactly* was the mole-hill—in the middle of the garden or where?" asked Robin.

"There was I dunno how many mole-hills in the garden."

"Did you mark the mole-hill where you found the sixpence—mark it with a stick or stone, or dig underneath it?"

"I'd more to do than dig up mole-heaps or put sticks on 'em, and I've more to do now." Mrs. Corderoy helped herself to another cup of tea. "Now, you've seen what you want, you'd best be off."

Marlene nearly spoiled everything by asking, "If you don't want the sixpence, can I have it for my collection?"

Actually, she had no collection of coins, but now seemed a good time to begin one. An Elizabethan sixpence would make a magnificent start.

Perhaps because Mrs Corderoy was a little deaf or perhaps because she had been stirring her tea so violently, rattling spoon against cup, she did not hear the question properly. Perhaps she was one of the many members of the "none-so-deaf-as-won't-hear club."

Anyway, she answered angrily, "Me give you sixpence for the church collection! I should think not indeed!"

"Not for church—for me."

"That's worse! I've known children put buttons in the church bag. I've known 'em change pennies into two halfpennies and keep half back from the bag. You started asking for sixpence, and then making out you only wanted to look."

"No, we didn't!" Robin jumped up, his freckled face nearly as red as his hair. "We came to look at that old sixpence so's we'd know what it looked like. We came to ask to dig for the treasure in your garden. If we find it we'll give you half!"

"Will you now?" A rather odd expression came over Mrs Corderoy's face: her eyes narrowed and her lips curved into a queer half-smile. "Will you now?"

"P'raps not now," replied Robin.

Rage was flaming inside him because Marlene had been insulted. She might be tiresome in a girl-like way. It had been stupid of her to ask for the Elizabethan sixpence, but she wasn't the sort of child who would cheat the church collection bag. If she were, he (Robin) would have had nothing to do with her. Visions of Spanish doubloons and golden Napoleons and pieces of eight and countless stores of Elizabethan sixpences slid out of his mind.

"P'raps not *now*!" he repeated. "P'raps we won't dig your garden now. Come on, Marlene!"

"Not so fast, now! Not so fast!"

Mrs Corderoy's face changed again. Now she looked less like a cunning witch and more like a poor, kind, old woman.

"You couldn't dig my garden over all by yourselves, little mites like you, could you, now?"

"We could try," said Marlene, though Robin kicked her.

"It would be doing a good turn to a poor old woman with a bad leg if her garden could be dug over. I'd get a lot more for the cottage if the garden were dug. And it'd seem more honest to leave the place nice for the next-comer when I go all electric."

"Then can we come and dig?" asked Marlene.

"That needs thinking over. I wouldn't want you to wear yourselves out for me: that'd never do. Happen you could bring some friends along to help?"

Before Robin could kick her again, Marlene had answered—"All us school kids'd come!"

"Ah!" Mrs Corderoy wagged a knotted forefinger. "But you needn't give back answers to me if you don't find treasure. There's no saying the treasure wasn't dug up afore my grandad's day."

But the sixpence? thought Robin.

Marlene spoke the three words aloud.

"Ah, but then you never know!" The forefinger was waggling again. "I'd be the last to want to deceive you. You come and see me in the morning, my dears, and I'll have thought what's best to be done. No, tomorrow's Sunday. Come along Monday ten o'clock time."

"O.K.!" said Marlene.

Robin felt as though he had run hot water from a cold tap, and cold water from a hot one; as though he'd bitten the sour half of a plum, and then the juicy half; and as though (a thing he enjoyed doing) he'd taken alternate sucks from a humbug and an acid-drop—one warming, the other icy cold.

"Oh! *Heck!*" said Robin, following Marlene down Mrs Corderoy's path.

He paused at the gate, and saw the old woman waving, waited until, not hobbling at all, she had hurried into her cottage.

Heck! thought Robin, walking away from Marlene, and

then jogging in the direction of Finch Cottage, which was his home. *Heck! It's not much of a cop being a 'tec, but I want to be a good one. Worzel Gummidge has done most of the finding out so far. Heck! It's a mean sort of job being a 'tec when criminals start being horrid and end nice. If I do find the treasure, I'll give the best part to Mrs Corderoy. I'll have a look at her back garden now.*

Robin hurried through the little snicket that led to a path dividing two cottages. The path ambled to the cart-track that ran along the foot of the Downs. He turned right and peeped through the elder hedge into Mrs Corderoy's garden.

As he looked, he nearly changed his mind about giving her nearly all the treasure because he saw that the digging would be very, very hard indeed.

The sight of an ancient, lichen-trimmed apple tree cheered him up. The tree was leafless and most of its boughs were dead and brittle-looking. Surely whoever had buried treasure would have marked the place. What better marker than an apple tree that must have been young and springy when the treasure was buried.

Or it might've been a pip, thought Robin, *a pip spat out by the burier; but that wouldn't be a good marker. He might have used an apple core if he'd meant to dig up the treasure soon. I must find out how long apples take to grow. Upsidaisy may know. Or the tree may have been hollow—a hollow tree'd be a good place for treasure. That tree looks hollow—wonder if I could nip into the garden and see.*

But before Robin could part the elder boughs, Mrs Corderoy came quite quickly into the garden. She was not using a stick, and she was not limping either. She hurried down the cinder path dividing what had once been vegetable beds, and then she took long strides to the hedge and back again, crossed the path, and repeated her strides to the other hedge.

That's funny, thought Robin; *it's funny her leg should be cured so quickly. She's walking like I did in London when I was dodging the lines between the paving stones. And yet she's not walking quite like that.*

A sheep-like cough behind him interrupted his thoughts. There, by a rotting haystack stood Worzel Gummidge and Earthy Mangold. Beside them stood an old plough, some bits of corrugated iron that had once been part of a pigsty, a chicken-coop and a tumbledown hen-house. The land belonged to the village carrier, who had done a little farming before he grew tired of it.

"Mornin'," said Gummidge, "We're scarin' mice and rats and spadgers and all sorts."

"It's not acos we minds 'em bein' here," explained Earthy. "They casn't do no harm where there's nothing *to* harm, but if we scares 'em away maybe they'll find more comfortin' homes for theirsels. Mrs Corderoy's cottage'd be cosier for the rats and mice and her thatch is a wunnerful place for spadgers' nest-buildin'."

"Ooh aye!" agreed Gummidge. "If they uses thatch they'll let me keep my straw stummick to itself, and not use it for nest-buildin'."

"Asides," Earthy spoke kindly as usual, "asides, the rats and mice'd be nice company for Mrs Corderoy in the evenings."

Hannah Harrow, the invalid scarecrow, raised herself from a truss of straw in a nettle-bed, and whined, "I've been a cruel sufferer from mice acos o' bein' stuffed with greengrocers' sawdust."

Robin, whose father had been a greengrocer before he

came to live in Scatterbrook, argued, "Greengrocers don't keep mice in sawdust."

"Not o' purpose maybe." Hannah Harrow raised a hand (once it had been a fruit-picker's hook) and brushed some strands of tarred bootlace hair back from her forehead. "Not o' purpose, but mice comes arter the grapes from foreign parts that's packed in sawdust. Then if ladies happens to get stuffed with foreign-parts sawdust, they suffers cruel from the mice same as I've done."

"You're not sufferin' from mice *now*, Hannah Harrow!" Earthy spoke almost sharply.

"I might start again—and rats, too. If rats and mice gets into Mrs Corderoy's bad leg, she'll be a cruel sufferer. Happens she'll suffer if they even *looks* at her leg, same as she does when humans looks at her. She suffers from a 'lookin'-at' disease, poor thing."

Robin was interested, and asked, "Does she——?"

"Time and again I've seen her whiles I've bein lyin' here on my bed o' sickness," moaned Hannah. "She hops about the gardin like a spadger and as soon's a human comes along the path and looks as if it might be goin' to look, Mrs Corderoy's leg goes all stiff and limpable."

"More like she's practisin' being' a scarecrow," said Gummidge. "Stands to reason we've *got* to have stiff legs differ nor humans. Humans'd do their own scarin' if we wasn't differ."

Hannah Harrow continued her invalidish chatter:

"I'd not be surprised if Mrs Corderoy's 'lookin'-at' disease is infectious. I feels me legs goin' bad. Give over lookin' at me, Earthy, afore I goes cripple."

Hannah Harrow was the only scarecrow to whom

Earthy ever spoke harshly, and now she snapped, "You'd enjoy it if you were crippled, Hannah Harrow, same as you enjoys all your ailments."

A bitterly offended expression came over the invalid scarecrow's face, and she whined, "Who's to enjoy me private ailments if I don't enjoy 'em mysel? There's nothin' o' me to enjoy excep' ailments. I'll not forget the first time you told me to look on the bright side, Earthy Mangold!"

Gummidge's wife blushed greenly, and she answered, "Nobody were more sorry nor me arter I'd said it."

"Hannah were!" contradicted Gummidge. "She looked on the bright side o' the village pond, and fell through to the mud."

"I were all of a miserable, soggy sog for days arter," wailed Hannah Harrow, "and a lot o' me mice came-to. The drownded ones stayed drownded, but the half-drownded ones gave artificial restoration to the mock-drownded ones, and they all started bein' mothers."

"But it were years and years ago, Hannah," said Earthy. "An' I said I was sorry till I dizzied. Casn't you forget it?"

"I've a fine mem'ry for sufferin'!" boasted Hannah. Earthy Mangold changed the subject—at least she changed it *in a way*:

"I happened to have a lady friend as were bright sides all the way round. She happened to be made o' canvas stuffed with cob-nuts."

"It's a wunner she didn't suffer from the squirrels!" interrupted Hannah shudderingly.

"Her stummick were pink linoleum, stuck on where the canvas happened to be tore. Very smart her stummick were. Ronnie Beeswax were her name."

"Beeswax's a polish." Robin was anxious to show knowledge, "Beeswax is a good sort of polish but Ronnie's a man's name."

"Her stummick *were* polished afore it were give to her, and her father were a he-scarecrow. She were named arter him."

"Stands to reason!" put in Gummidge.

Earthy continued her story.

"Ronnie Beeswax happened to be an allotment scarecrow—not schools, like Upsidaisy, but the big sort with huts and tool-sheds. The genelman she worked for had a rusty old bike that he kep' in one o' the sheds. One day a friend give him a big tin o' silver, shiny paint—bright as moonlight."

"Aluminium," put in Robin wisely.

"It were silver-shiny bright like moonlight, and one day when it were rainin' he went into the shed and painted his bike silver shiny. There were lots o' paint left over so he thought as how he'd smarten Ronnie Beeswax and make her silver shiny, so's she could work night-shift and scare the owls off of his allotment. So he fetched her into the shed and dried her wing feathers."

"Wing feathers?" asked Robin.

"Ronnie Beeswax happened to have wings acos a friend o' the genelman she worked for'd give him a stuffed eagle, and he'd took off the wings an' tied 'em on to Ronnie to make up for her not havin' no arms—very uncomfortin' it is not to have arms."

"If she'd wings," interrupted Hannah Harrow, "if she'd wings she'd be liable to all the hen diseases—roup an' gapes an' broody an egg-boundedness."

"Eagles is differ," said Earthy Mangold. "Eagles flies high."

"Then they'll have their own differ diseases—dizzies and giddies and dampness from clouds."

"As I were sayin'," Earthy spoke reprovingly—"as I were sayin', the genelman dried Ronnie's wings and face—her face happened to be made from a dinner plate that had a picter 'o a little girl painted on it. She'd blue eyes an' pink cheeks and gold hair same as Queenie Simmonds."

Robin shuddered.

"Very convenient it were to have a ready-painted plate for a face, though Ronnie's voice comin' from behind it sounded like chiny bein' smashed when dustbins is emptied. Well, as I were sayin', the genelman painted Ronnie—wings and stummick and canvas skin an' old umbrelly legs with the moonshiny paint. He left her face alone, 'cept that he give her silver eyebrows. Then, seein' as it had stopped rainin' and were gettin' dark, he put her out on the allotment to dry. She stood there all proud an' shinin' till the twins from the shop come along acos their Dad left his chopper in his shed and their mum wanted to chop firewood. They happened to come along just when Ronnie were spreadin' out her wings to dry, and flapping' 'em so that drops o' shiny paint was flyin' out like sparks o' moonshine. She happened to be chatterin' to herself in her breakin'-chiny voice. The twins rushed back screechin' that they'd seen the ghosteses o' giant hens in the genelman's allotment."

"Only one ghost," said Robin, who was trying to be very clever indeed that day and was practising his detective work. "Only one ghost if there was only one Ronnie Beeswax. If *I'd* been a 'tec and taking evidence from the twins I'd have asked——"

"What you asks is daft!" announced Worzel Gummidge. "Stands to reason, twins, since twins is *two*, sees and hears two times—that's arithmetic what I learned from Upsidaisy."

"As I were saying'," continued Earthy Mangold patiently, "the twins said as how they'd seen silver ghosteses. Their mum went to the allotment to look for hersel. Next night other humans went to look, but they was scared to go close to Ronnie acos she were chatterin' loud in her breakin'-chiny voice—that were acos she were lonesome acos nobody'd talk to her at night. Only the bell-ringer from the church were brave enough to go up to her.

"Next day he said to the genelman as kep' Ronnie's allotment, 'We've bats in the belfry at the church: they keeps comin' at us and flutterin' round when we're bell-ringin'. I'd not like to set up a norniary scarecrow on the church tower, but a nangel scarecrow same as yours, with shiny wings, could scare the bats reverent and church-like and stop 'em flitterin' round bell-ringers' faces."

"Bats is called flitter-mice!" wailed Hannah Harrow, "Mice as flitters is worse nor mice as scuttles. I do know that!"

"Hold your hush, Hannah, love!" said Earthy Mangold, "As I were sayin', the allotment genelman helped the bell-ringer carry Ronnie to top o' the church tower."

"That night she flapped her wings and stood up all shiny and chattered breakin-chinily agin the bats, but they all come at her, flyin' dartily and dodgin', like swallers arter flies."

"Ooh aye! Stands to reason!" remarked Worzel Gummidge moodily. "Bats allus flies to lamps an' lights an' angels: the bell-ringer were daft to think Ronnie could scare them."

"Bell-ringers were not pleased acos the bats still come at them so long as the light was on in the belfry. It weren't till arter lights was out that Ronnie suffered worse nor cruel. The more she flapped her wings the faster the bats came at her, flyin' round her shines and rushin' at her eyebrows and dodgin' past her stummick. She went daft in a week, poor soul."

"I suppose that's what they mean when they say a person's got *bats in the belfry* mused Robin, his detective mind hard at work. "Ronnie Beeswax went batty because of the bats in the belfry."

He laughed because it was fun to have discovered the reason for an expression.

"It weren't nothing to laugh at when Ronnie took to her umbrellas."

"What do you mean?"

"I *told* you as Ronnie had umbrella legs!" Earthy's voice was reproving. "Arter the bats'd sent her daft, she thought as how she were a bat hersel."

"That weren't daft, stands to reason, seein' as bats' wings is like umbrellas!" said Gummidge.

"Anyways, she took to her umbrellas and jumped off the church tower, but the umbrellas didn't open acos they was stuffed with rust and paint. Her wings fell off, acos they was tied on with rotten string. She fell onto the churchyard wall and broke her chiny face to little pieces."

A few sympathetic green tears rolled down Earthy's cheeks, and she continued chokingly: "She were set up again, but the umbrelly stuff sagged round her feet like Upsidaisy's ankle socks. One of her wings'd blown away in loose feathers, so she had to make do with one an' a washin'-up mop. The genelman as set her up again give her a new chiny plate face with a picture of a rabbit on it." Earthy's voice broke again. "I casn't abear to think of it. Very confusin' it were to Ronnie to think she were a bat and to have a face like a rabbit an' not be able to flitter acos she'd a mop-wing, and not be able to run acos the ankle socks was trailin'. The moonshiny paint wore off as the years went by, so she couldn't look on her bright sides no more. She must a been the saddest lady scarecrow in the world."

"She'd a won the prize!" said Gummidge.

"What prize?" asked Robin.

"Prize for the saddest scarecrow—stands to reason!"

Hannah Harrow peered hopefully through the straggles of her bootlace hair and asked, "Is there a prize for the saddest invalid?"

Robin did not wait to hear the answer, because frantic cackling sounded from Mrs Corderoy's garden.

He peeped through the hedge, and saw that she was chasing—yes actually *chasing* a black hen from among the brussels sprout stalks.

5
Treasure Trove

MONDAY MORNING was fine and sunny, and Mrs Corderoy's face was smiling as she opened the door to Robin and Marlene. Behind them in the village street stood a small army of children, carrying spades and forks, Tommy Higginsthwaite was swinging a pickaxe. Queenie held a toy watering can and a child's rake.

"Good morning," said Mrs Corderoy. "I've been thinking it over, and you're welcome to dig for treasure if you've a mind. You'd better come round to the back. I don't want a lot of muddy boots trapesing through my kitchen."

Robin led the way along the little path and through a gap between elder bushes.

A rocking chair and a footstool stood under the old apple tree. Lengths of string and wooden pegs divided half the garden into four-foot-wide strips, stretching from the hedge to the cinder path.

Robin plunged his fork into the ground beneath the apple-tree, struck a root and began to dig frantically.

"That's not the way!" said Mrs Corderoy. "You'll not find a lot of treasure if you dig like that."

She was leaning on her stick and hobbling down the path.

"I've marked out the garden—I mean I've had it marked out into strips—that way's fair to all."

The other children crowded round to listen.

"If you each take a strip and start at the hedge and dig backwards, you'll be able to see where you've been, and you'll not miss the treasure."

"But the hedge is all nettly!" whined Queenie.

"Ah, but I found my bit of the treasure right under a nettle-patch!" said Mrs Corderoy. "The treasure'll be worth more than a sting or two."

Robin stopped digging and looked up.

"I thought you'd found it on a mole-hill, that's what you *said.*"

"Nettles can grow on mole-hills, can't they?"

Robin was not at all sure that they could, but Mrs Corderoy's voice had sounded so sharp that he did not dare to argue for fear he should not be allowed to look for treasure.

In another five minutes all the children had begun to work. Robin and Marlene dug side by side. Tommy Higginsthwaite swung at the hard ground with his pick-axe. Queenie tickled the soil with the tiny rake and Norma worked with a weeding fork.

From time to time, Mrs Corderoy, who had settled herself in the rocking chair and propped her "bad leg" on the footstool, called out, "Dig deep! Dig deep if you want to find treasure!"

At first the excitement of competition made the children work hard: each was afraid that the others might be the first to find treasure.

Occasionally there was the ring of steel on metal, and the triumphant shout, "I've got it!" Then the children clustered, like terriers at a rat-hole, round the lucky digger until a bit of rusty barrel-hoop or the blade of a hoe or a kettle-lid or a tobacco tin was dragged up from the ground.

Tommy Higginsthwaite was envied by everyone because his pickaxe could go far into the heavy soil.

"It's not fair!" whined Queenie. "I've only got ever such a little rake. All of us ought to be the same."

"Dig on! Dig on! Dig on!" chanted Mrs Corderoy from her chair under the apple-tree. "You may be nearer to the treasure than you know."

Queenie scrabbled pettishly at the earth near an old cabbage stump, cried, "Got it! Gold!" and flung down her rake.

Robin was just in time to see the glint of shining metal as Queenie scooped up a quite new threepenny bit.

"Let's look! Let's have a see!" chorused the children.

"No!" Queenie's fingers closed over the coin. "It's mine!" Greedily, without bothering to look at the "treasure," she thrust it with half a handful of earth into her cardigan pocket. "It's mine!"

"That's right!" said Mrs Corderoy. "Finding's keeping! Where you find one, you may find more. Dig on! Dig on!"

Now, Robin, who because he had been digging the strip between Marlene and Queenie, had been the only one to see the threepenny bit, was very puzzled indeed. Mrs Corderoy could not have seen it from where she sat, so why had she not been more interested? Or could he have been mistaken in the shape and size of the coin? Was it gold indeed?

"Let's have a look," he begged.

Queenie tugged futilely at the cabbage stump, while the children gathered round her. For a moment, it looked as though Tommy Higginsthwaite was going to turn into a pickpocket, but Queenie's left hand did not leave her cardigan pocket. She gave up the struggle with the cabbage stump, and waved her rake dangerously.

"Let me have a peep," begged Robin, "just a peep because I know about treasure: I'm a 'tec."

"No! It's mine!" yelled Queenie.

"Go back to your strips!" shouted Mrs Corderoy fiercely.

"Go back to your places or you'll go out of the garden. You can't expect all the treasure to be in the same place. Dig on! Dig on!"

But you would expect all the treasure to be in the same place, thought Robin. *You would unless the treasure-burier was mad. Why wasn't the treasure buried deep?*

He glanced back at Mrs Corderoy, looking strangely witchlike as she rocked her chair and prodded the ground with the stick that should, he thought, have been a broomstick. Why had she not been more interested in Queenie's find, and hobbled over to look at it?

All the children were digging hard—all, that is, except Queenie who was tickling the surface of the soil with her little rake and working hard in her own way. Robin noticed that the cabbage stump had not been disturbed.

I'll come back at night, he thought. *I'll bring Dad's torch and I'll dig under that stump till I find the treasure.*

His thoughts were interrupted by a triumphant shout from Norma. "Gold! I've got it!"

Then the shout faded into a disappointed mutter, "It's only a silly old penny!"

"Let's look!" said Robin.

The penny was new and shining: it bore the pretty head of Queen Elizabeth the Second.

"And I'd been digging so hard," complained Norma.

"There was a great crack in the ground and I dug till I bent my spade."

Robin stooped down. Yes, there were cracks in the hard earth, stretching on either side of Norma's spade mark.

"P'raps someone dropped it," suggested Marlene.

"It was more than a foot deep," argued Norma, though the blade of her spade was less than that.

"Dig on! Dig on!" repeated Mrs Corderoy.

The children dug, but Robin's mind was working harder than his hands and feet.

The children went on digging. Marlene was happy because she found several old clay pipes. Some had broken stems and some had cracked bowls, but she decided to mend them and add them to her collection in the loft.

"Then," she confided to Robin, "Then some Sunday when the shops are shut, someone'll lose a pipe and not be able to smoke, and I'll sell him one of my pipes and buy baccy with the money, and then I'll start a pipe and baccy shop."

Mrs Corderoy hobbled into her cottage, and Robin took his chance of exploring the hollow trunk of the apple-tree. He hopped on to the stool, then on to the back of the rocking chair, and peered into the half-musty, half-sweet-smelling depth of the wood, but saw nothing but darkness.

I'll look with Dad's torch tonight, he thought. *Why does Mrs Corderoy sit under the apple-tree if she's not guarding treasure? Why didn't she want me to dig there? I'll bring a long pole with a hook—then if the treasure chest has a handle—*

The sound of an opening door made him hurry down from the chair. Mrs Corderoy, carrying a mug full of tea, was hobbling down the garden path. She settled herself in the rocking chair, and the children went on working.

From out of the corner of his eye Robin saw Queenie pick up her rake and watering can, and slink out of the garden. He wondered if she had found more treasure, and decided to follow her. He had just slipped through the hole in the hedge when he came face to face with Mr Dyke, the hedger and ditcher, who was his favourite man in Scatterbrook, and the only person who understood scarecrows.

"What's to do?" asked Mr Dyke.

Robin told him.

"Cunning old woman!" said Mr Dyke. "Mrs Corderoy's a cunning old woman right enough. You ask her if she'd like you to bring a dowser along to find the treasure. See what she says to that!"

"What's a dowser?" asked Robin.

"Water-diviners some call 'em, but they can find metal, too. There was a chap lived up on the Downs when I was a lad before all this fancy water was piped from the reservoirs, and the well-diggers was busy. This chap—his name was Harry Hawk—carried a forked hazel bough, one fork in each hand and the stem sticking straight out in front of him. He walked as slow as you do when you're going to school on Monday mornings. When he came on top of an underground spring, the hazel started acting like a mad thing, bending and turning and trying to twist out of his hands. Then Harry'd stop and say, 'Here's where to dig your well and find deep, sweet water.' He made a lot of money out of dowsing."

"D'you mean he found treasure?" asked Robin.

"Could've done if he'd walked over buried treasure, but folks paid him for finding water. My old Dad told me he'd go into the *Red Lion* of an evening, and the chaps'd blindfold him and hide money under the mats. Then

Harry'd take his hazel-bough and find the money every time. He'd no need to pay for his drinks, see!" Mr Dyke broke off into cackling laughter.

"Can anyone do it—be a dowser, I mean?" asked Robin.

"They say it's a gift, but I don't know the rights of it 'cept the twig must be hazel." Mr Dyke picked up his billhook. "Well, I must be getting along. You ask Mrs Corderoy if she'd sooner have dowsers than diggers. Cunning old girl!"

It was too late now to follow Queenie. Robin, hoping to find a hazel bush, hunted along the elder hedge. From its other side he heard the voice of Mrs Corderoy—"Dig on! Dig on!"

I may have the gift, thought Robin. *I may be a dowser and then I'll be the best 'tec in the world. I'll find where burglars and thugs have hidden their loot. If the Queen's crown's stolen, I'll find that AND the sceptre.*

He wished that, since he had not been born a country boy, he had been more interested in the botany lessons at school, because he was not quite sure of being able to recognise hazel.

" 'Mornin', my dear!"

Earthy Mangold's voice startled Robin, who had forgotten the scarecrows on the patch of waste ground owned by the carrier. Evidently, Earthy had listened to the conversation with Mr Dyke, for she plunged into one of her stories.

"I happened to have a genelman friend as happened to have hazel-bough arms and hands. His name were Hazy Loon and he was allus lookin' for water acos he were friendly with moles, and he thought he'd save 'em diggin' trouble. Very disappointin' it is for moles when they've been diggin' a long tunnel with their poor little feet, and they comes to a spring and the water rushes at 'em. Moles is so fat and their tunnels is so narrow they casn't turn back afore their feet and their noses is washed pink by all the water rushin' at 'em."

"Terrible suffers from colds in the noses and eyes and feet moles is," moaned Hannah Harrow from her bed among the nettles. "You've only to look at a mole to see how it suffers from colds in the head with its poor little, peepy, screwed-up eyes and its little red nose. Moles' colds goes to their feet and turns 'em same colour as their noses. Very infectious colds is—I suffered from a mole-cold the year afore last."

Robin remembered that the only mole he had seen had pink feet and a pink, wobbly nose and very screwed-up eyes.

"As I were sayin'," continued Earthy, "Hazy Loon were very considerate to moles. He used to walk about, bent half double, with his hands stretched down. Then, when he were above water, his fingers'd twitch and twist and he'd shout down to the moles, 'Don't you dig no further or you'll get colds in the heads and feets!' He worked for years till his fingers got permanent screwed and twisted and you couldn't hardly tell 'em from birds' nests."

"Ooh aye!" put in Worzel Gummidge, who had been lolling against the rotting haystack. "Ooh aye! I minds Hazy Loon. He grew benter and benter till he looked like a heron drinkin'."

"It were arter he grew so bent as the farmer that kep' him for scarin' thought he'd set him up on new legs. The farmer didn't notice as he was sufferin' from *waist*-bend, not leg-warps."

"Waist-bend's a sad disease!" groaned Hannah. "So's leg-warps, come to that."

Earthy continued hastily. "Hazy Loon's first legs happened to be made out o' the top bars of a garden gate. They was oak and the hinges was left on and fixed to his waist, which made bendin' easy for him. The farmer give him new hazel-bough legs to match his arms, and Hazy Loon set to work again. He thought as how his legs'd be very convenient for water-findin', and so they was when he first started. He strode about the medders, and his legs screwed and twisted all ways when they trod above water till he looked like Miss Dollit when she was teachin' the childers to dance round the maypole."

"Could he find treasure, too?" asked Robin. "Mr Dyke said dowsers *can*. Does Hazy Loon live in Scatterbrook?"

Earthy shook her head until green tears flew from her eyes to Hannah Harrow's bootlace hair, where they lay, sparkling like emeralds.

"Hazy Loon come to a sad end for such a kind mole-considerin' genelman. He went twistin' and writhin' and findin' water an' callin' out to moles till he come to the willow beds. The water there was too much for his poor legs, acos there was too much on it. His feet and legs went dartin' this way and that like midges in sunshine, and they kep 'twistin' and turnin' all restless till they screwed up in great big birds' nests. Mr Lay (him as kep' the willow beds and made baskets) happened to come along and find Hazy Loon."

Earthy shed a few more tears, and went on:

"Mr Lay happened to be makin' a lot o' baskets at the time, and he knew hazel was near as good as willow for basket-makin', so he untwisted Hazy Loon, and worked bits o' hands and feet and legs and arms into basket handles. Then he took the baskets to Dimden Market and sold 'em. They say he set up the *rest* o' Hazy Loon in the willow beds to scare the reed-warblers from makin' nests, but I've never had the heart to visit him. It's not nice to think about a considerate genelman friend goin' all differ ways at once in market-basket handles."

"He were daft to start with," argued Worzel Gummidge. "Stands to reason he were—else he'd not a let his arms and legs twist all ways at once like twitch-grass to stop moles catchin' cold. Stands to reason."

"Anyways, Worzel, love, it makes chattin' difficult!" Earthy Mangold spoke with dignity, "Hazy Loon and me enjoyed many a chat afore his accidents, but I casn't chat cosy with a genelman friend as is spread about in differ baskets in differ parts o' the Market!"

"You could follow him about," said Hannah. "You could follow him round, so long as you've the strength, and say a kind word here and a bad word there. Very infectious kind and bad words is."

A slow, obstinate expression came over Worzel Gummidge's turnip face. As Robin watched, he noticed that the scarecrow was stiffening. The muddy lips scarcely moved, and the words were mumbled: "It's enough to make anyone sulk. Stands to reason!"

"What stands to reason, Worzel, love?" asked Earthy.

"Hazy Loon," replied her husband. "Anyone'd think Hazy Loon's the only important scarecrow hereabouts!"

"So he WERE important afore he were spread about in baskets. It's not easy for little bits of a spread-about genelman to keep on bein' important."

"Anyone'd think as Hazy Loon's the only scarecrow as could find what's hid underground!" declared Gummidge. His broom-stick arms fell to his sides, his twiggy fingers creaked into silence, and the slits of his eyes narrowed.

"Sulks is infectious!" moaned Hannah Harrow, and flopped back into her bed of nettles.

It seemed to Robin that Earthy's next remark had nothing to do with the previous conversation.

"Earthworms needs a deal o' comfortin'!"

She was smiling indulgently at a small and very pink worm that had wriggled up through the earth at her feet.

Before the boy had time to say goodbye to the scarecrows, the children came teeming and tumbling through Mrs Corderoy's hedge.

"She says we've not to go back till tomorrow morning," said Marlene. "She says she's got to rest her poor legs this afternoon! Tommy Higginsthwaite found a halfpenny."

Ten hours later, and at exactly twelve o'clock, Robin was once again in Mrs Corderoy's garden. Luckily, his parents had gone to bed early and, even more luckily, his baby sister had slept soundly, not waking to cry out for a drink or for company. Robin had taken some stones and thistles to bed with him, knowing that if he slept a lump or a prickle would waken him. He had left a sharp spade and a hatchet outside the back door, and had hung a sack, for treasure-holding, on the pump handle.

Now he was ready to begin work. The wind was pushing clouds across the round, white face of the moon, and tossing the elder boughs so that they looked like dancing scarecrows. The old apple-tree cast wavering shadows on the ground. Robin wished the night was calmer, because the movement of the shadows and the creaking of branches made him feel jumpy. It was difficult to believe that the garden was not inhabited by all sorts of queer creatures. He glanced back at the cottage, but no light shone from the windows. He hoped that Mrs Corderoy was a sound sleeper.

It's all right, thought Robin. *I'm not trespassing. She said we could dig for treasure. She said, "Finding's keeping," but I'll share what I find.*

He crouched down by the apple-tree, and, because a teasing cloud was dawdling in front of the moon, switched on his father's torch. There was a hole in the hollow trunk, and it was about a foot from the ground and large enough to let a small boy's hand through—a hand only, not jacket and shirt sleeve, as Robin discovered when he pushed.

Off came the jacket, up went the shirt sleeve, and Robin tried again. The torchlight showed only the rotting wood of the opposite side of the trunk, and a few disgruntled insects. A beetle scurried downwards, a slater hid in a dusty crevice and a spider stared crossly.

Have to make the hole bigger, thought Robin. *I ought to muffle the axe so's not to make noise, but a muffled axe mayn't cut. I'll have a feel round first.*

He put down the torch and thrust his arm into the hole again, groping downwards, scraping his nails against bark, fumbling and prodding.

There WAS something in the hollow—something hard and cold, and not recognisably-shaped. Robin felt grittiness and smoothness as he tugged at the thing, which seemed to be wedged.

If I could get underneath it I could push it up, he thought, and, taking the axe in his left hand, he prodded with its handle against the rotting wood below his arm. There was a rending sound, his arm slipped down, and the wood turned into a trap. Robin tugged and twisted, but his arm was held tightly and painfully.

"Now WHAT?" he muttered.

It was then that the dreadful thing happened. Something or someone was walking very, very slowly down the cinder-path towards him. It didn't look like a man, but like a walking bush or bundle of pea-sticks. Then suddenly and maddeningly, as though a giant had turned off a sky switch, the moon went out. At least, that was how it seemed to Robin, though, of course a cloud was responsible for the darkness.

The torch was out of reach, and there was silence except for the shuffling of twigs among cinders. For a mad moment Robin wondered if one of the elder bushes had come to life and was taking an evening walk. Anything might happen on a night like this: the ancient apple-tree had behaved oddly, too.

The moon shone down again and its light showed the figure coming closer and closer.

"Evenin'!" said Worzel Gummidge.

The scarecrow's broomstick arms were stretched straight out from his shoulders, and he seemed to be wearing a mantle or shawl of pea-sticks. Their forks were caught on his arms, in the rags of his jacket and in his tarred string braces. His turnip face peered through a tangle of twigs.

" 'Evenin'," he repeated. "Hazy Loon's not the only scarecrow as can go dowsin'. I've been doin' it proper, and I won't get my fingers twisted neither. Mrs Kibbins has a good row o' peas growing in her back garden. She allus sticks 'em with hazel acos hazel's best. Peas resents elder and turns away from it. I helped mesel to pea-sticks this evenin' to show Earthy as Hazy Loon's not the only dowsin' scarecrow."

Robin forgot he was trapped, forgot the pain in his arm, forgot everything except his joy in seeing Worzel

"Wait a bit," begged Robin. "My arm's stuck in a hole"

Gummidge when he had expected something so much worse.

"AND I'm a 'tecative!" continued the scarecrow, "I knows where treasure's hid!"

"WHERE?" asked Robin, forgetting not to shout.

"Where she hid it—alongside of cabbage stumps—a bit here and a bit there an' all the bits where you'll be diggin' tomorrer. I seed her doin' it, but she didn't see me acos I were dressed up in hazel, and lurkin' in the hedge. She was chattin' to hersel while she were hidin' the treasure. 'A few coppers'll make the childers dig proper,' she says. 'It'd cost more nor a few coppers to get the gardin dug by a man,' she says."

Gummidge laughed the hoarse cackling laughter of scarecrows, and boasted, "I'm the best 'tecative hereabouts. I'm goin' back to tell Earthy. 'Evenin'!"

"Wait a bit," begged Robin. "My arm's stuck in a hole, and I can't get it out."

Creakingly, the scarecrow leaned forward, peered through the mask of hazel twigs, and said heartlessly, "What'll go in'll come out. Stands to reason! And what'll come out'll go in again."

"Beggin' your pardon, and if it's all the same to you, Worzel, love, what'll come out won't go back again."

Earthy Mangold had joined her husband on the cinder path, and was ducking through hazel twigs and under his outstretched arm.

"I know that, acos I happened to have a lady friend as happened to work in the *Red Lion* garden. I were visitin' her at the time, and she happened to find a sody-water siphon——"

"What's that?" interrupted Gummidge.

"It doesn't matter what it is!" snapped Robin, whose

arm had swollen and was hurting so much that he was in no mood to listen to stories. "It doesn't matter!"

"It mattered to my lady friend!" Earthy's voice was reproving. "A sody-water syphon's a big bottle with a big beak an' it's got a little pump-handle stickin' out o' the back of its neck, and when the handle's pumped, the bottle hisses like adders and spits fizzy water out of its beak."

"Stands to reason it's daft!" said Gummidge, and Robin wriggled his wrist despairingly.

"Well, my lady friend (her name were Dotty Swatter, acos her feet was made from fly-swatters) found the sody-syphon and pumped the handle and liked the spittin' and hissin' and says to me, 'That'll learn the adders to spit an' hiss at me!' She didn't happen to like adders, acos she couldn't spit an' hiss back at 'em—that was acos she happened to have a sunk-in mouth. Her head were a kicked-in football."

"Help!" said Robin feebly.

"It's not perlite to interrupt stories!" Worzel Gummidge told him.

"As I were sayin'," continued Earthy, "as I were sayin', Dotty Swatter kep' on pumping the bottle till all its spit were finished, and it gurgled DRY. Then she started tryin' to put the fizzes and the hisses back into the bottle. Very painstakin' she were, but she couldn't win. I left her sobbin' like a child. I had to leave her acos of a young beetle as needed comfortin'."

Earthy sighed, and ended her story. "So you see, Worzel, love, what comes out won't allus go back. Maybe what goes in won't come out neither."

She looked down at Robin, who said unhappily, "But I can't stay here all night!"

"Stands to reason you'll have to stay till the tree's felled or bonfired. Human childers is a deal too restless! That's a good, stout tree: it don't let go of its apples in a hurry—they stays on till November."

It was only April!

The years seemed to whizz backwards. Robin was not a brave and clever detective. He was not even a rather tough boy. He had become a child again, quite as helpless as his tiny sister, Mary Lou. It had been a disappointing day. Worzel Gummidge was THE detective of Scatterbrook. It was he who had discovered the secret of Mrs Corderoy's treasure, and it was hateful to be less important than a scarecrow. Robin leaned his cheek against the apple-tree, and longed for his mother.

Twiggy fingers combed his hair, and the gentle voice of Earthy Mangold sounded in his ear—the one that was not pressed against bark.

"Maybe I could wait alongside you till autumn, and do a bit o' comfortin'!"

The moon, that had been darkened for a few minutes, shone out brightly.

"Human tears isn't green same as mine!" said Earthy Mangold.

"Ooh aye! It's a good stout tree!"

Worzel Gummidge shuffled forward, raised a broomstick leg, and kicked at the shell of the apple trunk. Robin fell backwards. His right arm was freed: his right hand was clutching something cold and hard; it had a knobble at one end.

"A nugget! I bet it's a nugget!"

"'Evenin'!" answered Worzel Gummidge.

The scarecrow, now that his own work was done, was not interested. He turned his back, dropped his broomstick arms to his sides and, scattering pea-sticks, shambled away.

"You don't need no more comfortin', love," said Earthy, and followed her strange husband.

Then, before Robin could examine his find, another maddening cloud curtain was blown across the face of the moon. Robin groped for the torch, found the axe and the spade, dropped them both with a clatter, felt for the sack, and trod on the torch. By the time he had collected everything, hurt his wrist a good deal more, thrust torch and "treasure" into the sack, and stumbled over some pea-sticks, the cloud had passed on its way.

Two lights shone down, one from the moon, the other from Mrs Corderoy's bedroom. A window was flung up.

"Fire! Thieves! Murder! Help!" shouted Mrs Corderoy.

Noisily, as spade and axe clanged together, Robin crunched over the cinders, through the elder hedge, and into safety. Ten minutes later, he had reached home. Two minutes later, while his parents and Mary Lou slept, he was in his own bedroom, and had switched on the electric light.

It was not a nugget! It was an old bottle, so encrusted with greenish grit that Robin could not see if it were full or empty. It felt heavy, but it did not rattle, nor was there any sound, as he shook it, of plopping liquid. The cork had been driven home, and his finger nails made no impression on it.

Might be full of gold dust, thought Robin; *dust doesn't rattle or splash. If only the bathroom weren't downstairs I could wash it.*

He licked the glass hopefully, and the grit tasted old and musty, but somehow exciting.

Mum says a peck of March dust never hurt anyone. It's April now, but still——

He scrabbled in a drawer, found a clean vest and scrubbed and licked alternately.

Mum won't mind about the vest if I've found a bottleful of gold dust, thought Robin.

After a time, most of the greenish grit had left the bottle and clung to Robin's vest and mouth. He peered through the cloudy glass and saw the miracle inside—a three-masted ship, rigged, perfect, and no more than five inches long, sailed a greeny-blue painted sea. How, with its tall and fragile masts, had it gone through the narrow of the bottle-neck! Who had hidden it in the hollow of the apple-tree? Was it the true treasure of "Turkeys"?

If I was a good 'tec, I'd soon find out, thought Robin as he dragged off his clothes.

Then, all at once, the wish to be a detective slid away from him. Grimy-mouthed, grubby-handed, sore-wristed, sleepy-eyed, he scrambled into bed, held fast to his treasure and, dreaming of magic, fell asleep.

The many voices of the day and evening punctuated his dreams. *Dig on! Dig on! Dig on!* (Mrs Corderoy.) *It's mine! It's mine!* (Queenie.) *Cunning old woman!* (Mr Dyke.) *I casn't chat cosy with a genelman friend as is spread about in differ baskets.* (Earthy Mangold.) *Finding's keeping.* (Mrs Corderoy.) *What goes in'll come out.* (Worzel Gummidge.)

Could the ship come out of the bottle? Could it grow and grow? Ships—old ones—were made of oak, and oaks grew from acorns. Why shouldn't a tiny oaken ship grow, too? And *why* had Worzel Gummidge been dowsing when he knew where Mrs Corderoy had hidden the copper treasure? He decided to ask the scarecrow in the morning.

Hours later, Worzel Gummidge answered the question:

"I were dowsin' to show I'm the best dowser hereabouts—better nor Hazy Loon."

"But did you find anything?" persisted Robin.

"Ooh aye! Stands to reason!"

"What did you find?"

"A trousy button."

"But you weren't looking for trouser buttons!" objected Robin.

"It's best to look for what you finds. Stands to reason, if you've done that, then you've found what you looked for."

"Asides"—Earthy Mangold lowered her kind voice to a whisper—"asides, there's no hurt feelin's that way. If Mr Gummidge'd been dowsin' for Major Wazenby-Gunthorpe, supposin' Major Wazenby-Gunthorpe'd been buried in Mrs Corderoy's gardin', it wouldn't be kind nor perlite to show disappointment at the trousy button."

"Anyways," declared Worzel Gummidge, "anyways, I'm the best 'tecative hereabouts. I *seed* Mrs Corderoy hidin' pennies in her gardin so's to have it dug cheap."

"That's not being a 'tec!" argued Robin, "A 'tec finds clues!"

"I found a trousy button!"

"That's not being a 'tec," objected Robin. "That's being a witness."

Once again he tried to explain the methods of real detectives, but he knew his arguments had been wasted when Worzel Gummidge announced, "You can act daft and complicate and roundabout, but I'll know who dunnit! Stands to reason I'm the best 'tecative hereabouts."

Earthy Mangold smiled admiringly, Hannah Harrow moaned from her nettle-bed, a hen, chased by Mrs Corderoy, flew, screeching, over the hedge, and Robin went on his way.

A cat was washing its face outside the Post Office. Queenie, sucking a stick of pink Edinburgh rock, lolled against the notice-board.

"Mum gave me half a crown," she boasted. "And Gran gave me another to make up."

"What for?" asked Robin.

"For the gold being a threepenny—just a mean old threepenny. Did you find anything?"

"A ship in a bottle!" Robin had remembered his treasure, and the words burst out of him.

"Silly! A ship'd never get into a bottle!"

Robin hardly heard Queenie's whining voice. He closed his eyes.

"All right then, sulky!"

But he was not sulking: he was sailing. In his mind's eyes, which worked better when his real ones were shut, the cottages vanished into spray, the street turned blue and shiny as the glass of the bottle, and a pirate crew flourished their cutlasses.

I'll be a sea 'tec, thought Robin. *I'll be a sea 'tec. I'll find sea-chests of treasure and I'll tame an albatross and I'll find desert islands and I'll scuttle the enemy ships.*

6
The Hunt for Hannah

ROBIN AND MARLENE were at their usual meeting-place outside the Post Office. There was a new and exciting notice on the board.

Marlene read the words aloud:

"COUNTY COMPETITION

"*There will be a prize for the best-kept village in the county. Judging will take place during the months of April and May. Points will be awarded for general tidiness of roads, lanes gardens and the Railway Station. Well-kept hedges, and absence of litter in roads, on the Play Close and in the bus shelter will help to gain points.*

"*PLEASE help to make your village the pride of the county. Certificates will be given to the runners-up.*"

"I wonder what the prize will be," said Robin.

"P'raps they'll take us all to the cinema," suggested Marlene. "Or take us to the Zoo in coaches, or to the seaside or——"

She was interrupted by the opening of the Post Office door, and by the voice of Mrs Bloomsbury-Barton talking to Miss Dollit, "It will be most unfortunate if the judges happen to come round on dustbin day, when the village looks disgraceful."

"But people must have dustbins," argued Miss Dollit.

"There is no objection to nice, tidy dustbins with well-fitting lids, but so many people use old buckets and cardboard cartons and wooden tubs, stuffed to bursting-point with papers and litter that should be burned. Tins and bottles could be buried, and the bins should contain nothing but dust and ashes."

"Oh no!" breathed Marlene, for Tuesday (dustbin-emptying day) was her favourite in every week. Monday was her next favourite, because some people put dustbins outside their homes the evening before the collection was due. Marlene had found many a treasure for her store on Monday evenings and Tuesday mornings. It was wonderful what useful things were thrown away!

"I shall *speak* about dustbins at the next meeting of the Womens' Institute!" declared Mrs Bloomsbury-Barton. "And I shall make a point of examining every dustbin myself until the judging is over. You can help me, Phoebe."

"But *I* was going to address the Womens' Institute today!" objected Miss Dollit. "I was going to show the members how to cover match-boxes with sealing-wax. They look as though they are enamelled, and they make such pretty presents."

"Dustbins are more important than sealing-wax: so is the honour of Scatterbrook. Besides, sealing-wax match-boxes would be most dangerous—the wax would catch fire when the matches were struck."

"But a little excitement adds such fun to life!"

Mrs Bloomsbury-Barton did not answer. She stumped out of the Post Office, and Miss Dollit followed.

"Please," said Marlene, "please can I come and help you with the dustbins?"

Mrs Bloomsbury-Barton smiled at her. "I'm glad to see that you children are taking an interest in the village; but there are many other ways in which little people can help. You can pick up paper and cigarette packets from the sides of the road and in the bus shelter."

"Such helpful kiddies," put in Miss Dollit.

Robin was thinking: *I could be a 'tec when the judges come round. I could be a sort of backwards-way-on 'tec. If the judges are passing an untidy garden, I can point to a tidy one. I'd win the prize for Scatterbrook.*

Mrs Bloomsbury-Barton shattered his dream by saying, "The village should be tidied every day, because nobody knows when the judges will come."

"I could see to the dustbins by myself," persisted Marlene, but Mrs. Bloomsbury-Barton was speaking to Miss Dollit.

"We must ask the carrier to clear that untidy patch behind Mrs Corderoy's cottage. We must expect the judges to go everywhere, not only to the show bits of the village."

Robin decided that he had better warn the scarecrows, because nobody could think that Worzel Gummidge or Earthy Mangold or Hannah Harrow added to the tidiness of a village. While Marlene lingered hopefully, he hurried away.

Worzel and Earthy were in their usual places, but Hannah had left her bed of nettles.

"She's gone off for a change of air to cure her ailments," explained Earthy.

"Ooh aye! Stands to reason, she's daft," said Gummidge. "Air changes while you stands still, accordin' to the way the wind's blowin'. If she'd stayed long enough she'd a got a strong change o' air from Farmer Braithewaite's pigsties and Mrs Kibbins' hen-run."

"They do say as sea air's good for ailments, and sea air'd make a change for poor Hannah."

"There's plenty changes o' air when dustbins is emptied," answered Gummidge. "There's fish air and old-bone air and burnt-up-food air when dustbins is emptied and the wind's blowin' strong."

Earthy spoke gently and determinedly: "Beggin' your pardon, and if it's all the same to you, Worzel, love, change o' scent's not the same as change o' air."

"Stands to reason it is. Differ scents shows airs blowin' differ ways. When Hannah's east o' me and you're west, and wind's blowin' east, I smells her tarry hair. When wind's blowin' west I smells your face—old potato!"

Earthy looked so distressed that her husband added quite kindly, "There's worse scents nor old potato: old kippers from Mrs Kibbins' dustbin's worse. I've studied scents from dustbins since I've come down from Ten Acre."

The reference to dustbins had made Robin remember the conversation outside the Post Office, and he told the scarecrows what he had heard.

"Dustbins is daft!" declared Worzel Gummidge. "And those that fills 'em is dafter. What's the sense of takin' rubbige from one place and puttin' it in another? It don't make the world no smaller. There's a rubbige dump on the Downs alongside Ten Acre Field. The dustbin lorries empties tins there, and the dump gets bigger an' bigger."

"But wouldn't the village get smaller, love, if dust was all left there till the houses was covered up?" asked Earthy.

"Stands to reason it would, but the tin dump'd be

smaller. You casn't alter size by callin' it differ names. Scatterbrook'd be called *dump*, but it'd stay same size, only a differ shape, and differ sound, acos it'd be clattery to walk on."

Earthy's little eyes were full of admiration as she murmured, "You do think wunnerful, Worzel."

Her husband continued proudly, " 'Tis the same with human washin'-water. Humans gets water from pumps and washes the mud off of their clothes. Mud goes into the water an' makes the water fatter: clothes gets thinner. First, there's clean thin water and muddy thick clothes; then there's thick, muddy washin'-water and clean, thin clothes. What's the sense o' shiftin' dirt round the world and tirin' everyone out?"

Robin, remembering his mother's washing-days, when the kitchen was full of steaming clothes and the meals were not nearly so good as on other days, nodded understandingly. So did Earthy Mangold.

"I happened to have a lady friend as turned purple on a washing-day," she said. "Her name happened to be Beattie Bootleg—that were acos her face happened to be made from a big beetroot, and she wore a football boot. She'd only one leg acos she were a cripple. She were only a little bit o' a thing, acos her body happened to be short: it were made from a football, acos she'd been set up by a sportin' famly. Her boot'd been wore out by the youngest son—he'd lost the other one. Her body were one o' those long-shaped footballs."

"A rugger ball," put in Robin.

"As I were sayin'. Beattie Bootleg were only a little bit of a thing, but she were dressed smart, like me, in a sackin' cloak and skirt. Her blouse were made out o' a patchwork tea-cosy. She worked for Mrs Briggs, the washerwoman, an' one o' Mrs Briggs's grandchilders took a fancy to her, an' used to carry her in out' o' garden to be a comfort in her bed at night. It happened that Beattie's cloak were made out o' sackin' that used to cover a silo, and Mrs. Briggs didn't fancy the scent.

"One day when the water in the copper were still boilin', she said as she were goin' to give Beattie a good wash so's she'd be sweeter bed-company for Shirl, who were the grandchild. Shirl cried an' said she liked Beattie Bootleg as she were, but Mrs Briggs said, 'You'll like her better when she's wearin' a pale blue cloak and skirt. I'll put a lot o' washin' blue in the water'.

"Then she popped Beattie Bootleg in the copper, and give her a good boil-up. When she took her out to dry, Beattie were purple all over—face and clothes an' leg an' all. Shirl took a fancy agin her, acos she said she'd loved Beattie Bootleg as she *were* an' she didn't love her now she'd gone purple all over. Nobody couldn't unnerstand why a lady should go purple arter an hour's boil-up: it were a sad mystery."

Robin's detecting mind was at work. He remembered school painting lessons, and the ruby colour of beetroot-water after his mother had been boiling vegetables.

"Blue and red make purple!" he exclaimed. "When blue and red are mixed together, they make purple."

"Don't talk so daft!" snapped Gummidge. "You might just as well say that blue and yaller makes green!"

"So they do!" Robin's voice was triumphant.

"Haven't you never seen daffies an' forget-me-nots growin' all mixed up in Mrs Kibbins' gardin?"

"Yes, but——" Robin thought for a moment. "Blue and yellow has to be mixed with water before it turns into green."

"Stands to reason, rain's water, and there's plenty o' showers this time o' year. Don't talk so daft!"

Robin, tired of being called daft by the scarecrow, continued to argue: "I was talking about *paints.*"

"Beggin' your pardon, and if it's all the same to you, we was talkin' about poor Beattie Bootleg turnin' purple and bein' turned agin by Shirl. It's very akard for a lady to be the same colour as her clothes, and nothin' but the shape to show the differ. Asides——"

Here Earthy paused to shed a few green tears.

"Asides, Beattie Bootleg's head turned soft arter the boilin', so she didn't think so sensible as other scarecrows. She thought, 'I'd best seek company in purple company,' so she hopped away to a field o' pickling cabbages—very proud an' stiff they was. There weren't no chattin', but Beattie liked their company, acos they was the same shape as her stummick, so they seemed like relations. Then one day the short-sighted genelman as'd grown the cabbages come along and stopped by Beattie, and says, 'Here's a well-growed 'un,' and then he patted her head all friendly-like and then——"

As usual, when she was coming to the sad end of a story, Earthy's voice broke, and she finished sobbingly—"And then he said, 'This 'un's no use: it's gone soft on top!' So he threw her over the fence into a field an', an'—I casn't scarce abear to think on it—A COW ATE BEATTIE BOOTLEG'S HEAD. Arter that, she lost her memry. 'Twasn't her fault, poor thing, it were acos she happened to keep her memry inside o' the beet-root head, so it went into one o' the cow's stummicks."

"Stands to reason," said Gummidge. "Nobody'd want to remember bein' ate by a cow—not unless they was daft."

"She *were* daft arter that. I tried comfortin' her all ways I knew, but she weren't bright enough to 'member what I were comfortin' her *for*."

"Then she made a nice change from Hannah Harrow," remarked Gummidge unsympathetically.

Earthy shed some green tears, and sobbed, "I casn't even comfort Hannah now she's gone for a change o' air."

Robin, who was almost as impatient of tears as was Worzel Gummidge, decided to go to the railway station in search of Hannah Harrow, who might have decided to take a train to the seaside.

Mildew Turmut, the Railway Scarecrow, was in her usual place in the allotment by the signal-box. She waved to Robin when he came into sight. Waving came naturally to Mildew, because, instead of hands, she had red and green flags. She was wearing her everyday clothes—a porter's jacket, an old blue skirt and British Railway cup shoes. She had a window strap belt and, instead of a scarf, a towel with the words "British Railways" embroidered in red. A whistle was slung round her neck.

She did not trouble to say good morning, but began abruptly, "There's talk of closing the line to passengers, and only using it for goods. It shows what they think o' passengers. If they thought like that they'd call the passengers BADS, which they are, seein' as they calls the *things* GOODS, which they aren't always."

A few station sparrows flew down to peck hopefully at the lettuces. Mildew waved her flags at them, shouting, "All change! All change! Mind your backs!"

The sparrows obeyed swiftly and flew upwards.

"Have you seen Hannah Harrow?" asked Robin.

"She *were* here, asking for a train to *Sea Air* or *Change Air*, and said she'd got a ticket. Very fourth class Hannah is, and we don't run fourth-class carriages—only first and second and guards and goods. Very defrauding she is, too. She showed me her ticket——"

Mildew broke off to scare some more sparrows.

"She took the ticket out of her hair—a fifth-class place to keep it! It were a bus ticket to Dimden, all stuck up with tar, and it'd been punched to show it'd been used. I said to her, 'You're liable to a fine not exceeding five pounds for tryin' to defraud the British Railways,' and she said she didn't weigh as much as five pounds, and she couldn't spare herself. Mind your backs! Tickets, please! All change!"

A third flight of sparrows flew away, and Mildew continued:

"We were standin' by the weighing machine, and I shouted—'We'll soon see what you weigh! Mind your back!' Then I put her on the machine, and she sat there saggin'."

"What did she weigh?" asked Robin.

"Bert had hid the weights in the ticket-office to keep them safe from Tommy Higginsthwaite, who keeps on borrowing them for his aunt, who's trying to slim—that's what *he* says. I told him folks that's trying to unfat theirsels don't want weights to make 'em heavier."

"Where's Hannah now?" asked Robin, kneeling down to pull up some groundsel that was sprouting up between the lettuces. He had done so much gardening lately that weeding had become a habit.

"She might be in Dimden or she might be in prison for defrauding the bus company. You'll be in prison, too, if you don't put those weeds back; they're railway property! Stop bein' a defrauder." Mildew blew her whistle, and waved her red flag.

Robin answered angrily, "If this allotment isn't weeded, Scatterbrook won't win the prize for the best-kept village." Then, because Mildew lowered her flags and looked interested, he told her about the notice outside the Post Office.

The Railway Scarecrow pushed back her hair, which was made from the horsehair stuffing of old fashioned carriage seats, and said, "You can keep the weeds, then. I'll go along the line and scare the next passenger train off the lines. The Station would be tidy enough if it weren't for the passengers—all orange-peel and biscuit crumbs and lolly sticks and cigarette ends."

Whistling shrilly, the Railway Scarecrow left the allotment.

Robin might have followed, but his Aunt Ruby, who lived in Station Cottage, was calling to him from across the platform.

Anyway, he thought, *anyway, Mildew hasn't been able to scare a train off the rails yet. It'd be just my luck if she did it today when I wasn't there. If I was there and the train turned over, I might catch a criminal running away from cops. I'd know him by his handcuffs, because of being a 'tec. Or I might spot a rich old gentleman trapped under a carriage seat that nobody else had noticed and I'd drag him free before the train caught fire, and he wouldn't be just a rich old gentleman—he'd be a Chief Constable, and he'd beg me to go to Scotland Yard the second I've left school to learn to be a famous 'tec.*

"Robin! Robin!" shrilled Aunt Ruby.

"Aunts! Oh, heck!" muttered Robin.

Really, Aunt Ruby was not being at all "heckish". "I've steak and kidney pie in the oven," she told Robin, "and there's a jam roly-poly. Bert will take a message

"It's disgraceful!" said Mrs Bloomsbury-Barton, scrubbing away at the wall

to your mum to say you're stopping to dinner with me."

"Coo!" exclaimed Robin, and thought to himself, *I can still be a 'tec over Hannah, and I'll be nice and handy now if Mildew Turmut wrecks the train.*

The Scatterbrook bus shelter stood at one end of the village street, and was used not only by people waiting for buses but by those who liked to chat or gossip on rainy and windy days. There was a bench at the back, and two low walls in front. Framed notices, giving the times of buses, hung above the bench, and there was a litter-bin in one corner. Once a week, after the road-man had swept the rubbish from the floor, the bin was full, but on other days it was nearly empty.

Robin, who had enjoyed a very filling dinner with his Aunt Ruby, had hoped to reach the shelter before the afternoon bus to Dimden swept through the village. He had half expected to see Hannah Harrow sagging on the bench, but he was disappointed.

Miss Dollit was using a spiked stick to spear sweet-papers and cardboard cartons. Mrs Bloomsbury-Barton, a bucket of water beside her, was using a soapy flannel to scrub chalked words from the white-washed wall, which was used by the boys and girls of Scatterbrook partly as a Post Office, partly as a Notice Board but, more often, as a place on which to write rude remarks about their enemies. Some of the sentences, *T.H. is a beast*, *Shirl is a tale-tit*, *Go away, Queenie*, and *Meet me on the Green*, had been on the walls for months.

"It's disgraceful!" said Mrs Bloomsbury-Barton, scrubbing away at *Don't forget the bacon.* "It's absolutely disgraceful to write on walls!" So, indeed, it was, and Robin's parents would have agreed with Mrs Bloomsbury-

Barton, but it did make the shelter more interesting.

"Perhaps"—Miss Dollit straightened herself, and flourished the spiked stick—"perhaps, if we were to put books here—just paper-backs, and provide pencils and writing-pads (not for rude messages, of course), people would leave the walls alone."

"Don't be ridiculous, Phoebe, and don't wave that stick or you will pierce me! The books would be torn up, and so would the pads. Surely there is enough paper and litter as it is?"

"Yes, I'm afraid you're right!"

Robin, who had not been noticed, knew that Mrs Bloomsbury-Barton *was* right.

Miss Dollit continued to prod, and Mrs Bloomsbury-Barton to scrub, but not very successfully, for some of the sentences had been scrawled with nails, and were imbedded in the plaster.

"*Back soon*," read Mrs Bloomsbury-Barton. "That's been here since February. Now here's something quite new—*Gone Away—H.* It's written in red chalk, too: red only turns pink in water, however hard I scrub."

H, thought Robin, *H might stand for Hannah Harrow. I wouldn't have thought she could write, but p'raps Upsidaisy taught her.*

"*Run off to sea*," read Mrs Bloomsbury-Barton. "I do hope no child has been so foolish." She turned to Miss Dollit, and saw Robin.

"What a good boy!" she spoke approvingly. "So you have come to help us. Well, there's plenty to be done."

"And many hands make light work!" added Miss Dollit, spearing more paper into the bin.

Robin had seen something very interesting. There, at his feet was a stump of red chalk lying on a very crumpled bus ticket. He swooped down and snatched them up. The chalk was sticking to the ticket, and each was streaked with black. He lifted them to his nose, sniffed hard and was reminded of blackboards and the tarry smell of Hannah Harrow's hair.

"Coo!" he exclaimed, and sniffed again.

Mrs Bloomsbury-Barton, exclaiming, "Don't eat it, child!" snatched him by the arm. "You must never eat sweets that you find on the ground. You don't know *who* may have sucked them!"

" 'Tisn't a sweet: it's a clue!"

"Glue? That's even more dangerous!"

With a slurring of brakes, the bus to Dimden pulled up by the shelter. Two or three people bundled out, and Robin wrenching himself away from Mrs Bloomsbury-Barton, jumped in, and made his way to the back seat. At last he had the chance of proving himself. The finding of Hannah Harrow, though it was important that the scarecrows of Scatterbrook should be kept together, did not matter so much as that he (Robin) should find her, track her down by means of the clues, and show that he was a fine detective. In his pocket was a shilling, given to him by his Aunt Ruby, so he had money for his fare, and adventure lay before him.

As the bus drove away, he saw Mrs Higginsthwaite scurrying towards the shelter. As it gained speed, he noticed that she was waving her arms rather wildly, that Miss Dollit was brandishing her stick, while Mrs Bloomsbury-Barton shook her flannel.

Must've missed the bus, thought Robin, *but she needn't create all that much.*

He could not be very sorry for Mrs Higginsthwaite, who kept her son, Tommy, so short of pocket-money, and gave him such wretched meals, and left him to do all the washing-up and most of the house-work, too, while she went to the cinema. She was very different from Robin's kindly mother, who might be over-fussy about hand-washing before dinner and tooth-brushing at night, but who kept everything comfortable.

As the bus whirled on its way between the green hedges he made his plans. *I'll go to the station first,* he thought. *P'raps Hannah will be waiting on the platform. If she's not, I'll ask if any trains go to the sea and if a lady—well, a sort of lady—bought a ticket. But Hannah wouldn't have any money. She may have gone as a stowaway. I'll only have fourpence left from the return bus fare, so I can't follow her. Oh heck! I'll have to see what happens when I get there.*

Dimden was only a small station. It had four platforms, which were reached by stairs: the ticket office was down below.

"Yes?" said the clerk as Robin rapped on the glass window.

"Please, has anyone—well a sort of lady, sort of person——"

"Make up your mind!" snapped the clerk, cross because he had been interrupted while reading a letter from his cousin Mabel.

"Well, she looks like a scarecrow."

"Lost your mum?" The clerk smiled in the way some people do when they think they have said something clever and funny.

Robin went crimson with fury, but before he could think of a crushing reply he was prodded in the back by a market basket, and a woman, standing behind him said, "*If* you've quite finished!" and pushed past him.

Thinking that a porter might be more friendly, Robin rushed up the stairs, doubling between people who were coming down them.

"Ticket, please!" said a voice that might have belonged to Mildew Turmut, but did belong to a uniformed ticket-collector, who held out a hand.

"I only want to look for someone."

"Platform tickets in the slot machine just behind you."

Robin was rather fond of slot-machines, but he grudged the money for the ticket.

Hannah was not on the platform, nor in the Refreshment Room, nor in the General Waiting-room but Robin found a porter who was kinder than the booking office clerk and the ticket-collector, and not in such a hurry. Even he could not be helpful, for, after listening to the confused story, he explained that nobody could reach the sea without changing trains in London.

"She couldn't!" sighed Robin. "She's too *country*."

"Wait a bit, sonny," the porter pushed his cap to the back of his head. "I did see an old body that didn't know whether she was coming or going. She went into the Ladies' Waiting-room about half an hour back."

A train puffed into the station, the porter hurried towards it, and Robin dashed into the Ladies' Waiting-room.

There, slouched on a bench, a shapeless hat half hiding her face and half covering straggling hair, *was* "an old body"!

"Hannah!" shouted Robin.

A head was raised and the eyes of a very old gipsy, who often sold clothes-pegs in Scatterbrook and Dimden, blinked sleepily at him.

7
The Major's Best Clothes

"HECK!" THOUGHT ROBIN as the bus rattled on its return journey from Dimden to Scatterbrook, "Heck! It's not much cop being a cop!"

He had wasted a shilling on a fare, a platform ticket and a stale bun. He had searched Dimden and had not found a single clue. He was surprised to find Miss Dollit and Mrs Higginsthwaite waiting in the bus shelter as he (the only passenger for Scatterbrook) jumped down on to the pavement.

"He's not with you, then? You've not found him?" asked Miss Dollit.

"Did you see him?" asked Mrs Higginsthwaite.

"Her", corrected Robin, wondering how anyone could know that he had been in search of Hannah.

"Dot's at home: it's Tommy that's run away. We thought you'd gone after him."

"Because of the writing on the wall!" Miss Dollit, who was carrying her spiked stick, now used it to point to the red-chalked words in the shelter—*gone away—H* and *Run off to sea.*

"He left a note on his bed—same red writing, but it said '*Run away for good*'. He went before he'd had a bite of breakfast. Dad and me had a bit of a lie-in this morning because of going to the pictures last night. Dot found the note after she'd brought me a cuppa at twelve o'clock time. (Dot was Tommy Higginsthwaite's sister.) I had a bit of a wash and cooked myself some rashers and put some chips to warm up for Tommy, but he never came back for dinner."

"But," asked Miss Dollit as Mrs Higginsthwaite stopped for breath, "but weren't you worried after you'd seen the note?"

"I thought he was having me on because we'd had words last night—he'd broken a dish when he was washing-up while I was at the pictures, and he'd thrown it in the pig-pail along of his supper."

"Then he must have been feeling ill," said Miss Dollit. "A *well* kiddie would never throw a nice supper away, would he, Robin?"

"Dunno what his supper *was*."

"Bread and marge and plenty of it, and he's the sauce to say the bread was stale crusts and the marge was train-oil."

Once again, Robin had turned into a detective. "H doesn't stand for Tommy, and '*Gone away*' is signed 'H.'"

"H is for Higginsthwaite. Tommy wants to be called Higginsthwaite because he says he's the man of the family and Tommy's a name that's only fit for vegetables."

Robin nodded, remembering the days when his father kept a greengrocer's shop, and people asked for "half a pound of *tommies*." Perhaps each tomato blushed for shame at being described as *tommy*. Possibly other vegetables suffered, too—artichokes, known, so often, as *arties*, and cucumbers, *cues*.

Miss Dollit was talking to Mrs Higginsthwaite. "I

can't understand why you didn't worry *more* when Tommy didn't come home for his dinner!"

"Worry? You should've seen me worrying and trembling. I had to sit down to a good strong cup o' tea, and then the chips started burning in the oven and I thought, 'I'll go to Dimden and buy more fish and chips for poor little old Tommy,' and then I missed the bus and you told me about the writing on the wall, so I knew it was true and Tommy had run off to sea. He'll be a cabin boy now—tossing on the waves and tempests and longing for the sight of his old mum."

"Nonsense!" For once Miss Dollit spoke as sensibly as though she were Mrs Bloomsbury-Barton. "Nonsense! I don't suppose Tommy is very far away, but you and I had better tell the policeman. Robin, dear, if you see Tommy ask him to go home at once."

"And tell him all's forgiven and forgotten!" declared Mrs Higginsthwaite. "And tell him to finish the washing-up and feed the hens and make the beds, because Dot'll have gone round to Gloria to have her hair done."

"O.K!" agreed Robin.

He decided to visit the scarecrows, Worzel Gummidge and Earthy Mangold, before going home. There was just a chance that Hannah Harrow might have changed her muddled mind and returned to Scatterbrook.

If not, he thought, *if not there'll be two people to track. I may find them both together. When you find a marble, you often find another one you'd lost days ago. Wish they weren't going to the police. They might have left it to me.*

When he reached the waste ground at the back of Mrs Corderoy's cottage, Earthy Mangold came half-hopping, half-shuffling towards him. Her face was streaked with green tears.

"Oh, Robin, love!" she sobbed, "Mr Gummidge is in his sticks, and he's been sulking since Mrs Kibbins' hens started cackling early this morning."

"In his sticks?" repeated Robin.

"His clothes have been took off of him or blowed off of him, and he's in his broomsticks and shirt. He'll never be able to flap at crows no more, acos his shirt fits tight acos o' his stuffin'. Maybe you can unsulk him, seein' as I casn't."

Earthy hopped towards Hannah Harrow's old nettle-bed, and Robin followed. There, hatless, coatless, trouser-less, sat Worzel Gummidge, propped against a bale of rotting straw. A few green shoots sprouted from his turnip head, and his eyes were closed. His faded blue shirt fitted so tightly that his straw stuffing stuck out from between the buttonholes.

"His stummick'll be a prey to every nest-building spadger. I'll have to spend the rest o' my life spadger-scarin' or he'll be a skelington soon, seein' as spadgers nest all the year round!" wailed Earthy.

"Why are his lips red?" asked Robin. "*And* his cheeks? They used to be turnip-coloured."

The Scarecrow's lips were smeared with red, and looked much longer than usual—one corner was turned up, and the other down. One reddened cheek was higher than the other.

"It didn't seem nice to have a husbin' sulkin' in his sticks so I dressed his face as the human ladies in Scatter-brook dresses theirs," explained Earthy. "I found a bit o' the stuff they uses."

With the toe of a bottle-straw boot, she prodded a stump of red chalk that was lying by Gummidge's broom-stick leg.

"A clue!" shouted Robin as he pocketed the chalk, "A fine clue! Have you seen Tommy Higginsthwaite?"

"Beggin' your pardon, and if it's all the same to you," Earthy spoke reprovingly, "It's my husbin as is sulkin' in his sticks and not Tommy Higginsthwaite. I do needs comfortin' when I think how smart Mr Gummidge used to look."

Certainly, the scarecrow did not look smart now. His shirt had only half a tattered sleeve on the right side. His tarred string braces dangled limply and his bottle-straw boots stuck up from the polished broomstick ankles.

"Gummidge!" said Robin. "Mr Worzel Gummidge!"

There was no reply, and no sound except for a slight rustling of straw under the scarecrow's shirt.

"That's only a mouse havin' a run round in Mr Gummidge's stummick," explained Earthy. "It's the *same* one!"

"Same what?" asked Robin.

"Same mouse as I were comfortin' when what happened to Mr Gummidge happened, and me not there to see what happened. I'd heard a mouse squeakin' by the haystack, so I went along to comfort it. It were piebald and it were the smallest o' the family and the famly'd taken a bit o' cheese-rind off of it. It'd found the cheese-rind itsel, so natural it were squeakin' pitiful and cross, and it took a lot o' comfortin'. I found its brother and took a bit o' cheese-rind off of it, and then the piebald mouse turned pertickler and wouldn't fancy cheese with other mices' nibbles, though the nibbles was all in the same famly. By the time I'd comforted its appetite and hushed its squeaks and gone back to Mr Gummidge, there he was in his sulks and sticks."

Earthy looked sadly down at her husband, "Oh, Worzel, love, please to come to."

"Burning feathers bring people out of faints," said Robin, remembering the stories of his grandmother. "They might cure sulks. You burn feathers and hold them under the person's nose and——"

"The very idea!" squealed Earthy. "It'd be very comfortless to set light to spadgers!"

"Not sparrows!"

"Hens'd feel worse, seein' there's more o' them to feel."

"Not live feathers—moulted ones."

"Birds has a right to their own moults same as Mr Gummidge has a right to his moulted clothes."

Earthy turned her back on Robin, and addressed her husband. "Oh, Worzel, love, you puts me in mind o' the smartest lady friend I ever knew."

He doesn't look smart, thought Robin.

"This lady friend o' mine—her name were Twiggy Bustle first time—were dressed plain and simple in a yeller sating cloak and a strawberry-punnet hat and a red white and blue skirt made out of a old flag. She worked in the Vicarage kitchen gardin. One Christmas, the childers o' the Vicarage took the thought to dress her like a fairy and put her in a tree they was decoratin' for a birds' Christmas party.

"They took her plain clothes off of her and dressed her up all wild and fluffy in tissy paper, and called her Tissy Rustle, and stuck her in a tree along o' the birdseed and coconuts an' fat. They'd give her a smart pink-and-white face that'd come off of an old doll an' only had the nose melted.

"The birds' party went on a week or more, and when all the fat had been beaked up, the bluetits started on

Tissy Rustle's face an' beaked an' beaked till there were only her old face left behind it. Her old face happened to be made out o' a stockin' foot stuffed with rags, and not very startlin'. Arter the party were over it started snowin' an' the snow sogged Tissy Rustle's new white clothes till she were left in her sticks same as you, Worzel, love!"

Still, there was no sign or sound from the red-lipped, red-cheeked scarecrow, sitting at his wife's feet.

Green tears dripped from Earthy's cheeks as she continued: "When spring come, Tissy Rustle were blowed out o' the tree and lay in her sticks till the gardener come along an' says to the Vicar, 'That's just the job I need to fill that gap in the orchard hedge,' an' he takes her away. Oh, Worzel, love, give over sulkin' afore the Vicar's gardiner comes along. I casn't abear to think as I'll have a hedge-stoppin' husbin!"

There was no response and, as the green tears were flowing faster, Robin thought it was time for him to go away. The stub of red chalk was in his pocket, and his chance had come—at least, it would come next day.

Robin was not allowed to begin the morning by being a detective because it was dustbin-day, and his mother, who had been to the evening meeting of the Women's Institute, was determined that her bin should be the pride of the village.

"You look after Mary-Lou," she said. "Keep her out of mischief and keep her away from the bonfire."

So while Mrs Elliot wrapped tins into tidy parcels, made a bonfire for burnable rubbish, and even polished the outside of the dustbin, Robin played with his baby sister.

At eleven o'clock, while blue wisps of smoke curled up from the little bonfire, Mrs Bloomsbury-Barton appeared at Finch Cottage. Marlene tagged hopefully behind her.

"What a pretty garden, Mrs Elliot!" said Mrs Bloomsbury-Barton, "and how beautifully the hedge is trimmed. I'm sure you won't mind if I just peep into your dustbin, though I'm certain it isn't necessary."

Mrs Elliot stood back proudly while the shining lid was removed and the pleasant scent of carbolic rose from the bin.

"A perfect example to the whole village!" declared Mrs Bloomsbury-Barton as Marlene sniffed sadly. "Scatterbrook would be sure to win the prize if all the dustbins and gardens were as tidy as yours."

While she was replacing the lid, Major Wazenby-Gunthorpe, followed by his spaniel, Dinah, stumped up the lane, paused, and glared at Mrs Bloomsbury-Barton.

"So it's true!" he said. "I could scarcely believe Mrs Kibbins when she complained to me, as a magistrate. Perhaps you will have the goodness to return my suit!"

"Your s-suit?" stammered Mrs Bloomsbury-Barton.

"My best—er—my favourite suit. The gardener told me he'd seen my wife stuffin' it into the dustbin early this morning. Now she's gone to London, and my suit's gone *somewhere*! Puttin' two and two together, I conclude you are responsible."

"I d—don't understand, Major Wazenby-Gunthorpe. Why should I know anything about your suit? I don't remember——"

"Then let me refresh your memory in case you don't remember takin' Mrs Kibbins's hats and—and other articles of clothing from the side of her dustbin!"

"Certainly I remember," Mrs Bloomsbury-Barton drew herself up. "Certainly I remember moving a bundle of hats and rags from outside Mrs Kibbins's cottage, and asking her to put them on the bonfire because they looked so unsightly."

"Bonfire, eh?" Major Wazenby-Gunthorpe sniffed. "Bonfire! Beg pardon, Mrs Elliot."

He opened the garden gate and, followed by Dinah, strode towards the little bonfire, and returned angrily.

"Not a shred left if it has been burned. Women are all the same! The trouble I've had with that suit. Time and again I've bought that suit back from jumble sales when my wife's tried to get rid of it."

"B-but I thought you said it was your best suit!" bleated Mrs Bloomsbury-Barton.

"So it is—my best for gardenin', my favourite suit. Old clothes *are* best!"

Suddenly, Major Wazenby-Gunthorpe noticed Robin, "Oh! It's you, boy! You know old clothes are best, don't you?"

Robin grinned his answer.

Mrs Bloomsbury-Barton said, "Major Wazenby-Gunthorpe, I can assure you that I have not seen your suit and I have not been near your dustbin."

The Major grunted grudgingly, "Must take the word of a lady, but my advice to you is not to go interferin' with dustbins: it's not legal. Question is what's happened to my suit—that's the question. Come on, Dinah!"

Robin's mind had been at work. He remembered stories he'd read about tracker-dogs. Now he spoke his thoughts aloud.

"Please," he said. "Please, sir, Dinah knows your smell and she knows the smell of your suit——"

"ROBIN!" Mrs Elliot's voice was horrified, "ROBIN, mind your manners!"

The man and the boy understood one another.

"Grand idea! First-rate! You take Dinah along—she'll go with you if I tell her—and if you and she find my suit I'll give you half a crown. Here, Dinah, good lass—you go along with the boy!"

Major Wazenby-Gunthorpe took a leather lead from his pocket, fastened the shackle to Dinah's collar, put the loop into Robin's hand, and said, "Good luck, boy!"

The spaniel's stumpy tail wagged, her black body waggled and her pink tongue came out to kiss Robin's face. He was the proudest boy in the world.

I've got three things to find, he thought as he raced towards the village, *Hannah Harrow, Tommy Higginsthwaite and Major Wazenby-Gunthorpe's clothes. I've the chance of being the best 'tec in England. Coo!*

Dinah tugged at her lead. It was her way of showing that she wanted to explore the hedge and ditch that lined one side of the road. Her tail wagged, her body waggled and her nose quivered as she thrust it between tussocks of grass.

"Good lass!" said Robin, imitating Major Wazenby-Gunthorpe.

Now he was not leading, but being led by the dog. A blackbird started from the hedge, a stoat ran across the lane, a pigeon rose on clattering wings, but Dinah's nose did not discover anything important on the way down to Scatterbrook.

In the hope that Hannah Harrow might have returned to her bed of nettles, Robin took the path that led past Mrs Corderoy's cottage. Dinah sniffed excitedly at the haystack and wuffed at Earthy Mangold, who stood disconsolately alone.

"Mr Gummidge's deserted!" she said. "He's deserted

in his sticks. If he'd only give me warnin' I'd've give him the lend o' my cloak."

"When did he go?" asked Robin.

"If I'd known that I'd a gone along with him. He must a went while I was tryin' to stroke a hedgehog's bristles forrard. The hedgehog were tryin' to back backards into the rick, an' its spines kep' stickin'. It takes a long time to stroke a hedgie's bristles forrard and it weren't grateful neither. It pushed 'em about all ways at once, an' then it ran forrard and scuttled into the ditch without so much as a kindly word. Arter it'd gone I seed Mr Gummidge'd gone. Farmer Braithewaite'd just brought his cows down for milkin'."

"It must have been early this morning," said Robin, thinking, *That's four things to find.*

"Early or late, what's the differ seein' as Mr Gummidge's deserted me? I casn't seek him, acos he'd not have no home to come back to suppose he did come home and me not there to welcome him. I happened to have a lady friend as suffered from a desertin' husbin, and she wore her walkin'-stick legs to half their startin' length trampin' the Downs in search of him. She dwarfed her legs, poor lady. Her name were——"

But Dinah was tugging at her lead, and Robin was not in the mood to listen to scarecrow stories.

"We'll find him!" he boasted. "Come on, Dinah!"

The Downs were most exciting to the spaniel—as exciting as a thrilling book. Indeed, to her they were a dog's book, and she read it to herself as she wriggled and wagged and sniffed—"A leveret lay here, a covey of partridges got up from there, a nasty bad hedgehog—WUFF——"

Suddenly she put down her nose and, following an

invisible trail, stretched her lead, and tugged Robin along. There was great urgency in her quivering body as she and the boy skirted a little copse, and found themselves at the back of three white-washed cottages.

A haystack stood behind them, and in front of the haystack were two moving figures. Dinah yelped and tugged. Robin recognised Worzel Gummidge's old black hat—this was on one of the heads: on the other was a familiar tweed cap.

Then a maddening thing happened. A fly, in the tiresome way of flies, and choosing the worst possible moment, flew straight into Robin's right eye. At the same time, Dinah's jerk at the lead brought him to his knees in a muddy puddle, and water splashed up into both eyes! Through a blurry mist he *thought* he saw Worzel Gummidge pursuing Major Wazenby-Gunthorpe. Knuckling muddy water from his eyes, Robin looked again.

By now, both figures were coming towards him, and he was reminded of windmills! The black-hatted one came first: his arms were stiffly aslant. He hopped, as though trying to win a sackrace (this was because the trousers, looking like a couple of concertinas, were so much too long for his short legs) and he won it.

"Save us!" said Tommy Higginsthwaite as he stumbled forwards to share part of the puddle with Robin.

The second figure was not far behind: he had not hopped, he had shambled. His broomstick arms, in Major Wazenby-Gunthorpe's old tweed jacket, stuck straight out from his shoulders, and a tweed cap was askew on the turnip head. Bottle-straw boots peeped out from below shabby tweed trousers.

"Gimme my smart clothes!" said Worzel Gummidge.

Robin, his right eye smarting still because the fly had not left it, blinked again, disentangled himself from the lead, and struggled up from the puddle.

"What's happened?" he asked.

Interrupting and contradicting each other, Tommy Higginsthwaite and Worzel Gummidge told their stories while Dinah sniffed ecstatically as Major Wazenby-Gunthorpe's sagging trousers. Tommy had changed his mind about running away to sea—partly because he had not enough money and partly because he was afraid of the world beyond Scatterbrook.

"I thought I could be a sort of tramp," he explained. "And live rough and get a sort of living from turnips and scraps from dustbins and hen-food and such. And then I saw the old scarecrow thrown away behind Mrs Corderoy's, and I took its clothes to be a disguise."

"Don't talk so daft," muttered Worzel Gummidge. "Stands to reason I weren't throwed away. I'd throwed mesel into a sulk."

Dinah was barking so excitedly that Tommy did not hear the scarecrow's words, and continued his story.

He had written his messages on the wall of the bus shelter, so that nobody should search for him in Scatterbrook. After finding the scarecrow and taking his clothes, he had taken a hedge stake and pushed it through the arms of Gummidge's jacket.

"I was doing fine," he ended. "I'd found some eggs from a hen laying wild and I'd had some potato peelings and slept in a barn. I was doing fine till the Major started chasing me round the haystack. I'd not meant to do *him* any harm."

Tommy glanced nervously at Worzel Gummidge, who had turned his back and was stiffening proudly.

"Please, sir," begged Tommy. "Please don't send me to prison. I'd sooner go back to Mum."

"She wants you back," said Robin. "She said so."

"Stands to reason, she's daft!" The words came from Gummidge, but Tommy glared at Robin, and answered, "Daft yourself! She's *my* mum when all's said and done."

Very slowly, Worzel Gummidge creaked round until he was facing the boys.

Now Major Wazenby-Gunthorpe was a red-faced man, but his cheeks were level and his mouth was straight. Also, his eyebrows matched.

"Save us!" whispered Tommy to Robin. "What's come over the Major?"

"He's not the Major!" whispered Robin to Tommy. "He's a scarecrow!"

"Save us!" repeated Tommy. "I'm going back to Mum!" Clutching the too-long trousers, he tried to run, but tripped.

"Go where you likes!" shouted Gummidge, "but you'll not go in my smart clothes. I didn't happen to be needin' 'em when you took 'em off o' me. I'm not the selfish sort—not like that dog i' the manger as grudged the cow hay it didn't fancy for itself acos its teeth were differ. Asides, you was interruptin' me best sulk. It's imperlite to interrupt sulks—it makes the sulks go deeper. Stands to reason!"

Tommy's right foot had gone through a hole in Gummidge's right trouser leg, and this made running away impossible.

"I sulked a bit and come to a bit, as is *right* for sulks," continued Gummidge. "Last time I come to, me broomsticks was lookin' lonely—missin' their smart covers—so

I took a walk round the dustbins. Dustbins is best places for findin' smart clothes——"

Robin interrupted, "Did you go to Major Wazenby-Gunthorpe's bin?"

"Stands to reason—*arter* I'd been to Mrs Kibbins's, but straw hats don't dress a genelman—not proper, and there was only hats in the bin—hats as would a suited Earthy or Hannah——"

"Have you seen Hannah?"

"Time and again—on and off for years."

"I mean today?"

"There were a muddle in Mrs Marbles's dustbin as *might* a been her." Gummidge pointed towards Tommy. "Gimme my clothes!"

"Save us!" said Tommy. "These Downs aren't safe. I want my Mum!"

Hindered by Dinah, Robin helped Tommy out of the scarecrow's old trousers and jacket, took the hat from his head and flung the hedge stake to the ground.

Gummidge looked on moodily as the boy shook some mud from his shorts and pulled some wisps of straw from his grubby jersey.

"You've stole some o' my stummick!" he said.

"Save us!" yelled Tommy, and bolted towards Scatterbrook. Dinah, lead trailing, feathery ears flapping, bolted in another direction—towards her own and much-loved master.

Major Wazenby-Gunthorpe, golf-bag slung from his shoulders, was approaching Worzel Gummidge from the rear.

"Hi you—you fellow!" he shouted, "What are you doing in my suit?"

"Heck!" muttered Robin. "Oh, heck!"

Dinah, yelping for joy, was ranging between her master and the scarecrow.

"Answer me, fellow. Confound your impudence!" panted Major Wazenby-Gunthorpe. He strode forward, and tapped Worzel Gummidge on the shoulder.

"What the——? Why the——? Answer when I speak to you!"

Mercifully, the scarecrow stiffened into a firm sulk. There was a rustle of straw, a creaking of wood, but no reply.

Then Major Wazenby-Gunthorpe noticed Robin, and demanded, "Is the fellow mad? What are you doing here?"

For once the right and only answer popped into the boy's mind, and he replied, "Please, sir, I've found your clothes—at least Dinah did. And, please, he's not a fellow."

In another few moments, Major Wazenby-Gunthorpe and Worzel Gummidge were face to face. The scarecrow's eyes were closed, his right eyebrow bristled and the green shoot of a turnip top peeped coyly from under the tweed cap.

"A scarecrow, by George!" Major Wazenby-Gunthorpe glared suspiciously at Robin, "Did you dress it up in my things?"

"No. We—Dinah and me—just found him."

"Must've been one of the other lads, then. Thought he was being funny, I suppose. Oh, well, I've done worse things myself as a lad. We'd better get my suit off the thing."

"I'll do it. I can manage!" Robin spoke desperately, for what would happen if Worzel Gummidge came out of his sulk while being undressed by Major Wazenby-Gunthorpe?

"Sure?"

Robin nodded. He was not very sure, but somehow he would *have* to manage.

"Then you can take the suit down to my house. Better hand it in at the back door. Don't want my wife to see it. She wouldn't fancy my wearing the cast-offs of a scarecrow. You know what women are!"

Pride and fear battled in Robin's mind—pride at being addressed as from man to man—fear that Worzel Gummidge might come out of his sulk and lose his temper. (He heard the faint creaking of a broomstick arm.)

"Not that she need be so fussy," continued Major Wazenby-Gunthorpe. "Did you ever hear the story of that clergyman fellow who lived in a village not far from Scatterbrook?"

No, thought Robin, *and I don't want to hear it—not now when Gummidge is ready to come out of his sulk.*

"His name was Blewbury Jones, and he was a miser." Major Wazenby-Gunthorpe planted a foot firmly on to the crown of the scarecrow's old hat that was lying on the ground by Robin.

Again came the threatening creak of broomstick limbs and the rustle of straw.

"Yes; he was a miser. He cadged most of his food from the people in the village because he was too mean to spend his own money. One day, he came across a scarecrow, standing in a field. Its coat wasn't so ragged as this Jones fellow's, so he whipped it off, and wore it for the rest of his life."

Go away! Go away! Go AWAY! wished Robin, for the creaking was becoming louder.

"What I mean is why should my wife be fussy? If a

rich clergyman fellow could wear a scarecrow's coat, why shouldn't I have my favourite suit back?"

"Stands to reason!"

The familiar voice spoke the familiar words.

Robin wished he were a rabbit and could bolt into a hole, but Major Wazenby-Gunthorpe beamed at him.

"Of course it stands to reason. You're a sensible lad—most sensible I've met for a long time."

"Stands to reason!"

"You needn't sound so cock-a-hoop about it! Just take that suit to the back door. You'll find half a crown in one of the pockets—that is if the old scarecrow hasn't pinched it!"

Major Wazenby-Gunthorpe laughed loudly and strode away, followed by Dinah.

He was only just in time, for, rustling and creaking, Worzel Gummidge came out of his sulk.

"Stands to reason, he's daft. Ooh aye!" he raged. "Daft and imperlite *and* he's trod my smart hat flat as a mushroom! I'll not demean mesel to wear his clothes. Gimme my coat."

Undressing and dressing a stiff, sulky and obstinate scarecrow must be one of the most difficult things in the world. Gummidge's bottle-straw boots stuck in the holes of his trouser legs, his twiggy fingers caught in the sleeves of his coat, and the hat, which he insisted on wearing before he was dressed, kept falling off his determined head.

"I put my cap on *last*!" protested Robin, picking up the hat for the sixth time.

"Stands to reason pigeons wouldn't fancy eatin' the sprouts o' your hairs—not if they was pertickler," said Gummidge rudely.

"There aren't any pigeons about."

Just then two of these birds, with a clatter of wings, flew from one of the cottage elms.

"Maybe you think them's spiders!" said Gummidge.

Robin felt almost too cross to answer. He bundled Major Wazenby-Gunthorpe's suit together and set off for Scatterbrook. Worzel Gummidge followed creakingly.

I've found Tommy Higginsthwaite, thought Robin, *and I've found Major Wazenby-Gunthorpe's clothes and I've found Worzel Gummidge. I'll find Hannah Harrow by myself without Dinah or anybody.*

Now, sad—very sad—to say, a big rubbish dump spoiled a bit of the Downs above Scatterbrook. There, rats raced amongst potato peelings and pushed their noses into tins. There, tramps changed their old boots for slightly newer ones, and searched for treasures that might have been thrown away by mistake. Every dustbin-day, the lorries lumbered up the Downs, and added their horrid loads to the dump.

Robin and Worzel had nearly reached the village when the boy noticed the lorry drawn up by the side of the wide track. The driver and his mate were eating their dinners on the bank some little way from the vehicle's huge bonnet.

Robin hurried by, stopped to take a stone out of his shoe, and was overtaken by Worzel Gummidge. (Perhaps the dustbin men were too used to the sight of strange, untidy objects and fluttering rags to have taken any notice of a walking scarecrow or, perhaps their eyes were dimmed by the dust of the Scatterbrook bins.)

"Thought as you was lookin' for Hannah!" remarked Gummidge. "I thought as how you'd've took a interest in her hair, seein' as you likes to 'tecative all roundabout and complicate!"

Robin straightened himself. There, dangling from one

of Gummidge's twiggy fingers was a tarred string bootlace. Undoubtedly it was a lock of Hannah's hair, and it was grey with dust.

"Where did you find it?" asked Robin, but before Gummidge could answer—though he might not have answered at all—a faint screaming sounded from the back of the lorry. Hannah Harrow's basket hat tumbled over the tail-board. Her sad face peered down. Her bootlace hair was as grey as the faded locks of Mrs Kibbins. By the tail-board stood Earthy Mangold.

"Oh, Hannah, love," she kept repeating helplessly.

"I've got the old ages!" moaned Hannah as Robin rushed up. "I've just had a peep at mesel in a tin-lid, and the change o' air's give me the old ages. Me smart hair's as grey as Mrs Briggs's."

"It's only dust," Robin told her, "It'll wash off."

"Mrs Briggs is allus washin'." That was true for Mrs Briggs was the village washerwoman. "An' she's not washed her old ages away. Change o' air's a horrible disease. Help me down."

As Robin and Earthy tugged and hauled and Hannah's legs rattled among the tins and bottles, Worzel Gummidge asked, "Was you in Mrs Marbles's dustbin?"

"I were havin' a nice fold-up change o' air an' rest, an' Mrs Bloomsbury-Barton peeped at me an' told Mrs Marble her dustbin were a disgrace, and clanged the lid down. I were tryin' to get out acos I didn't want to catch the disgraces, an' then, an' then I were tipped into this moty car. The things," moaned Hannah, "the things an' dust an' the ashes that were tipped on top o' me! I don't fancy going' to the seaside in this moty-car."

"Now then! Now then!" One of the dustman had come up to Robin. "Leave those things alone. They become

Council property as soon as they're tipped into the lorry!"

"I don't like this moty-car: it's not dainty!" moaned Hannah.

"Save us!" said the driver, who had joined his mate, "It's an old woman! How'd she get here?"

"Stowaway, eh?" said the mate. "You wouldn't think an old body like that'd have the nerve."

"I'm a invalid!" moaned Hannah proudly.

"Not your mum?" asked the driver.

Robin shook his head indignantly.

"Know anything about her—where she lives?"

"Yes; in Scatterbrook."

"Looks to me as though she ought to be in hospital."

Hannah beamed at him, and murmured, "You're a very unnerstannin' genelman."

"We'd best have you out of here," said the driver and, catching hold of Hannah, he swung her down. "She don't weigh much more than a bird-cage."

"Stands to reason, she's daft!" declared Worzel Gummidge.

"Relation of yours, is she?"

For answer the scarecrow glared, turned his back and shuffled towards Scatterbrook, closely followed by Earthy.

"D'you think we ought to fetch a doctor?" asked the driver.

"Dunno," replied the mate.

"That's a wunnerful thought!" said Hannah. "I been a cruel sufferer."

Robin, who could not think what would happen if prim and perky Dr Moon came to visit Hannah, said quickly, "I can look after her. I'll take her back to Scatterbrook. I know where she lives and everything."

"There's a good lad!" said the driver.

Luckily, the walk back was very short. Half-dragging, half-carrying the sagging Hannah, Robin found Worzel Gummidge and Earthy on the waste ground behind Mrs Corderoy's cottage.

"Oh, Hannah, love!" exclaimed Earthy, "You do look differ!"

"I'm sufferin' from the old ages, an' I'm sufferin' from change of airs and Council-properties an' disgraces from Mrs Marbles's dustbin *an'* grey hairs!"

"Ladies with grey hairs gets treated with respecks," consoled Earthy.

Hannah Harrow almost smiled through the tattered tangles of her grey bootlace hair.

"Anyway," said Robin, "anyway, I was the 'tec who found her!"

"More's the pity you did, but you'd not a found her if I'd not seed one o' her hairs lyin' about all careless. It was me as found the clue. Stands to reason, I'm the best 'tecative hereabouts!"

8
The Heron Scarer

KIND MISS ARMITAGE, who was known in the village as "The Cruelty Lady" because she worked so hard for the R.S.P.C.A. and spent most of her time finding homes for kittens and taking other people's dogs for walks and seeing that tame rabbits were shaded from the sun and that their hutches were kept clean, had bought a new house. This was because the bungalow in which she used to live was too small for her *and* the many birds and animals she rescued from unkindness, and kept as *un*paying guests until she could cure their injuries and settle them into happy homes.

The house was new only to her: actually, it was one of the oldest in the village. At the back there was a big tangle of garden and a small paddock. There were sheds and stables, too, and there was a goldfish pond, surrounded by concrete, and full of gleaming, darting life.

Miss Armitage had spent a happy winter. She had made rabbit hutches, turned the stables into kennels for stray dogs, petted many a kitten, and loaded her bird-tables with food.

When spring came, she knew that the garden needed more help than she could give it.

"Either I must neglect it or neglect my creatures," she said, "and I can't neglect *them.*"

"Then you must have a gardener," Mrs Bloomsbury-Barton told her.

"I suppose so, but not a proper gardener like your Mr Dodgson. You see, I must keep groundsel for the canaries, and chickweed for the chicks. Proper gardeners are much too fond of weeding and pruning, and they're angry when puppies scratch in seed beds."

Mrs Bloomsbury-Barton snorted. "Certainly Mr Dodgson would not suit you, Miss Armitage. I think you need a zoo keeper!"

"But the Zoological Gardens in London are so terribly tidy. I want my garden to be only a little tidier than it is. The trees are beginning to meet, but I must have some hiding-places, rubbish heaps and long grass for the hedgehogs. I'm worried about the pond: the goldfish are getting no sunshine because of the overhanging branches."

Mrs Bloomsbury-Barton snorted again, and said, "Perhaps the Labour Exchange in Dimden could find you a suitable man."

The conversation took place in Miss Armitage's tangled garden. Robin and Marlene were there because they had been helping to cut the tufts of matted hair from behind the ears of a shabby and neglected cat. Robin had done most of the work. Marlene had been cleaning out the budgerigars' aviary and had made a collection of tiny brilliant blue and green and yellow feathers. She hoped to sell them as hat-trimming to Gloria of the Post Office.

The next morning, Miss Armitage bicycled into Dimden. The morning after that Mike Savage came to work for her. He was tall, dark-faced, dark-eyed, dark-haired, and he moved as silently as a cat. The only noisy thing about him was the clankety-clanking bicycle which was to rattle him from Dimden and back three days a week.

Robin and Marlene were in Miss Armitage's garden when Mike Savage arrived for his first day's work. They had been collecting dandelion leaves for rabbits.

"He looks like a poacher my Grandad knew," whispered Marlene to Robin. "His name was Savage—Sam Savage—and he lived in a shack on the Downs when he wasn't in prison."

P'raps Mike Savage is a poacher, thought Robin. *I'd like to catch one. I hate their beastly snares. P'raps Mike's a brother of Sam. I'll have to find out.*

Miss Armitage was talking to her new gardener, and explaining his work. She told him not to pull up any groundsel or chickweed or any of the seeding grasses loved by budgies.

"I dote on birds," said Mike Savage.

"Then we shall get on splendidly."

Miss Armitage told Mike to prune the overhanging branches of the trees on one side of the little pond because her goldfish needed sunlight as well as shade.

"I dote on fish," said Mike, but he winked at Robin in a way the boy did not like because Miss Armitage was a kind, nice person.

She continued to give her instructions. The grass was to be cut, but not too short, because mice and hedgehogs needed safe hiding places.

"I dote on animals," said Mike, but he winked again.

In a fortnight's time Miss Armitage's garden was looking tidy, but not too tidy. The goldfish had sunlight as well as shade, and their scales looked brighter than ever. Miss Armitage counted them every day. At least she counted the big ones, and there were twenty-four of them;

the small ones were too numerous and too swift to be countable. Mike had told her, and this was true, that some goldfish are cannibals and eat one another. The thought distressed Miss Armitage.

One sad morning, four of the biggest goldfish were missing.

"It's just like I said," explained Mike. "They've turned cannibal."

"But goldfish couldn't swallow *bigger* goldfish—they could *not.*"

"You'd be surprised!" said Mike. "Once they start they'll go on—that's the way of cannibal fish. You only need one cannibal in a pond, and the rest'll go in no time."

Three days later, three more fish had vanished.

"It's just like I said!" Mike spoke triumphantly. "Once you get a cannibal in a pond there's no stopping it."

"You could watch," put in Robin. "You could watch, and then catch the cannibal fish. Marlene and I could take it in turns to watch. We'd be 'tecs."

"What kind children!" said Miss Armitage. "What very kind children. Perhaps you could catch the cannibal fish in a butterfly net. Then it would have to live in a big tank by itself. I hate those horrid little glass bowls."

"O.K.! We'll be 'tecs!" exclaimed Robin.

Mike Savage looked as savage as his second name, but he spoke quite pleasantly—even sadly:

"That'd be no good. Cannibal fish won't *cannibal* while they're watched."

We could hide in the apple-tree, thought Robin, *in the one with the branches overhanging the pond. The fish wouldn't see us, and we'd cop the cannibal. That's what we'll do.*

They hid in a branch of the apple-tree overhanging the pond

That is what he and Marlene did for most of that sunny Saturday afternoon, and for a great part of Sunday. They lay on the lichened boughs, sucked sweets, and peered down through the leaves at the goldfish swimming peacefully in their pond.

"P'raps they don't cannibal on Sunday," remarked Marlene on the afternoon of the second day. "P'raps they're as good as gold then." She giggled, but Robin thought his thoughts.

On Monday morning when Mike Savage had come to work, Miss Armitage counted her fish. Not one of the big ones was missing.

"We watched them!" said Marlene. Robin kicked her, but too late! "We watched, and they were all as good as gold."

"Arh!" Mike Savage's voice was triumphant. "What did I say, now? Fish won't cannibal while they're being watched."

"But we hid: they couldn't see us."

"Fish smells!" declared Mike Savage. "Fish smells as cunning as a whippet on the scent of an old Jack hare."

"Really?" enquired Miss Armitage, "I had no idea of that. What a lot you know about country life."

"I dote on it!" Mike Savage smiled at Miss Armitage, scowled at the children, and walked slinkily away.

On Tuesday, five big goldfish were missing.

"Might be a heron," said Mike Savage after Miss Armitage had remarked that she could not understand why cannibal fish did not look twice the size of their companions.

"Yes," agreed Robin, "Marlene's fatter than me. If I was a cannibal and ate her, I'd be twice as big as I am, and I'd weigh twice."

He felt proud of his arithmetic until Mike Savage smiled at him in a pitying sort of way, smiled more humbly at Miss Armitage, and said, "Herons can gobble fish as soon as look at 'em. I saw a heron in the water-cress beds only last Saturday morning when I was biking back from work. It was eating tiddlers by the score."

Then Miss Armitage remembered, and remembered aloud, the story of a friend whose pond had been emptied of goldfish by a hungry heron in two or three days until she thought of borrowing a scarecrow, and putting it near the pond.

"A fine idea!" agreed Mike Savage. "Now, that is a fine idea. A scarcecrow'd be more use than a pack of noisy children." He glared at Robin and Marlene. "Scare-crows keep quiet!"

"I can find a scarecrow—a 'tec scarecrow!" shouted Robin.

That afternoon Hannah Harrow sat in a deck-chair by the side of the goldfish pond. She was a sad and shabby figure. Worzel Gummidge had refused to be a heron-scarer and Earthy declared she would only be a heron-comforter. "They needs comfortin' acos they've got such long swallows. I'd a lady friend once as happened to have a long swaller. Her neck happened to be made from a length o' hose-pipe—long as a heron's neck—and her head were a goldfish bowl. Her legs and arms was made from chestnut fencin'. She wore a brown paper vest, and her name was wrote on it in blue letters—her name was Ferty-Liza. She'd a blue nose an' blue eyes and blue cheeks an' a blue mouth acos the genelman she worked for had painted her face on the goldfish bowl.

"The genelman were a market-gardener and he set her up in a dahlia bed. She'd two jobs—scarin' bud-peckin' birds, and catchin' earwigs. Some gardeners puts flower-pots on sticks to catch earwigs, but Ferty-Liza's genelman liked his garden to look smart. She happened to have boots made from bits o' crazy-pavin, but the sad thing was she'd never seen 'em, acos she dursent bend her neck for fear her head'd drop off of it, acos the rim were a loose fit. No lady as had blue lips an' cheeks an' eyes an' nose'd want 'em browned by fallin' on to earth, an' Ferty-Liza was most pertickler. She didn't mind scarin' the bud-peckin' birds, nor she didn't mind the earwigs scutterin' up her legs an' inside of her vest and up the outside o' her neck, but she minded the tickle inside o' her long swaller. She couldn't use her swaller proper, acos the hosepipe were so stiff. The earwigs noticed as she couldn't swaller proper, an' when they'd run down they run up. They kep' on runnin' down an' up an' down an' up an' down till Ferty-Liza got the tickle-giggles."

"Very infectious tickle-giggles is!" Hannah Harrow interrupted from her bed of nettles.

"She giggled till she cracked her face, an' then her head went off of her. She were never the same arter that. Her genelman give her a new head made from a candle-lantern. He give her a new painted face—yeller eyes an' yeller lips an' yeller cheeks an' a yeller nose, but he lit the candle inside her head, so the moths come at her an' tickled worse nor earwigs, acos o' havin' more fluttery wings. I casn't say what happened arter that acos the genelman sold the market-garden when I happened to be visitin' Mildew Turmut. I often thinks sad thoughts about Ferty-Liza an' I've allus pitied herons for havin' such long swallers an' havin' to eat long wriggles."

So Hannah Harrow became the Scatterbrook heron-scarer, though, as she sat, grey-haired, sad and crumpled, in Miss Armitage's deck chair, she did not look as though she would have strength or spirit to scare a midge.

"The herons'll get used to the scarecrow," Mike Savage told Miss Armitage. "So will the cannibal fish. You mark my words!"

"I hope you're wrong," said kind Miss Armitage. "But you've proved yourself a good prophet so far."

"I believe *he* takes the goldfish," whispered Robin to Marlene.

"Why would he want them, silly?" whispered Marlene to Robin. "They're no good to eat."

"Anyway, I'm going to sleuth him!"

So for the rest of the afternoon Robin collected enough dandelion leaves to feed a hundred rabbits and, when not doing that, followed Mike Savage, and asked a great many questions, such as: "How would you catch a goldfish? What's a prison like inside? Could you eat a goldfish?"

Always the replies were the same—"How should I know?" and "What are you getting at?"

One of the many outbuildings belonging to Miss Armitage was a disused wash-house with a copper and a fireplace. Mike Savage ate his sandwiches there, and he seemed to be a very slow eater. On this particular afternoon he went to the wash-house even earlier than usual, and slammed the door in Robin's face.

The boy wandered about, fed the rabbits, played with a family of five long-haired white kittens, and then visited Hannah Harrow.

The invalid scarecrow was staring at the pond and opening and shutting her mouth continually. "I've got the gulpy-gobbles," she explained between gulps. "I've caught 'em from the fish. Very infectious gulpy-gobbles is, and very wearin' out to mouths!"

Looking at the goldfish, Robin noticed that they were opening and shutting their small golden lips and waving their tails.

"I'll catch the slithers soon, I shouldn't wonder," gulped Hannah. "Very infectious the slithers is—you've got to be wet to slither proper like fish, and if you're wet you catches croup. I don't know how I'll manage croup and gulpy-gobbles at the same time!" She pulled her shawl more closely round her, and continued to gulp silently.

Robin tried to count the baby fish, but they moved too quickly, so he wandered back to the wash-house, and peeped through the cobwebby window.

Mike Savage had not begun to eat his sandwiches, they lay in an open carpet bag. The man was kneeling by the fireplace. With an old flue brush he was sweeping soot from the chimney into a big cardboard carton. It seemed an odd occupation for a gardener.

Presently Robin could bear his own curiosity no longer, and he opened the wash-house door. Mike Savage jumped up, dusted soot from the knees of his trousers, and shouted angrily, "What do you want *now*?"

"Are you going to light a fire?"

"No, I'm not."

"Then why are you sweeping the chimney?"

"Soot's good for gardens," replied Mike. "It's good for lettuces."

"There aren't any lettuces, the rabbits have eaten them."

"That's not to say there won't be any." Mike had hesitated before answering the last question. Now he seized Robin by the collar and bundled him out of the wash-house.

"What are you getting at?" he shouted, "Why are you always snooping round?"

But, thought Robin as the door slammed behind him, *he wouldn't mind me snooping if there was nothing to snoop. What's soot got to do with goldfish? Heck! It's no cop being a cop.*

Miss Armitage, who was wheeling her bicycle towards the back door, called out, "Isn't it splendid! I think I've found homes for all the white kittens!" From the folds of a red cardigan in her bicycle basket a small white face peeped out. "I took this one round as a sample, and six people fell in love with it because it's so fluffy. Really, it looks almost Persian."

Mike Savage walked slinkily out of the wash-house.

"Just been having my bit of tea," he remarked.

Then you've been very quick! thought Robin, noticing that the man kept his hands in his trouser pockets, and wondering if he wanted to hide their sootiness from Miss Armitage.

"Pretty little thing," said Mike, looking at the kitten, "It's a shame about white cats!"

"What is?" asked Miss Armitage.

"Terrible wanderers," replied Mike, "Soon as the kittens start running about they're off—poaching, maybe—you can't seem to keep a white kitten at home."

"Oh dear! I never knew that." Miss Armitage sighed. "I hope these kittens won't run away now that I've found such happy homes for all of them."

"You mark my words!" Mike Savage spoke gloomily. "You keep an eye on those kittens, and shut them up at night. When did you say they're going away?"

Miss Armitage had not said, but now she answered, "Not till the end of the week."

"The wash-house would be a good place for them: the door shuts close. They'd be safer there than in the shed. I could rig up a cosy basket for them."

"How good you are!" murmured kind Miss Armitage. Turning to Robin she told him that she had met his mother in the village and that he was to hurry home to tea because his parents were taking him to the Dimden cinema.

"I think it's a special treat," she said. "A special treat because I told your mother how helpful you have been to me."

"It's not my place to mention it," said Mike Savage, glaring at Robin. "I hope you'll forgive the liberty, but I don't think children running about do birds and animals any good—they get rough with them."

"Robin and Marlene are very gentle indeed." Miss Armitage spoke firmly.

"Just as you wish, miss. I only thought I'd mention it."

All the way home, Robin puzzled. Ordinarily the cinema *would* have been a treat, and he knew that a Western was being shown at Dimden. Nevertheless, he would rather have stayed in Miss Armitage's garden until Mike Savage had bicycled home.

Why didn't he want me to see him sweeping that chimney? he thought. *What has soot got to do with goldfish?*

9
The Prophet

"THE SCARECROW is the greatest success!" announced kind Miss Armitage when Robin visited her next morning, "I've just counted the big goldfish and not another one is missing."

"How are the kittens?" asked Robin.

"Splendid! Mike Savage settled them in the wash-house last night. Really, I don't know what I should do without that man. He thinks of everything. There are two more scarecrows in the orchard. I suppose Mike made them or brought them yesterday evening. You remember he said that the heron or the cannibal fish might get used to a scarecrow. I expect he means to ring the changes—and use a different one. Isn't that a clever idea?"

Robin nodded, but not very certainly.

"Just count the goldfish again will you, dear—just in case I've miscounted. You'll feed the rabbits, won't you? I must go now. I hear Mrs. Rowstock is keeping her new puppy tied up for far too long."

Miss Armitage bustled away, and Robin visited Hannah by the goldfish pond. She was suffering still from "the gulpy-gobbles". Her lips were streaked with yellow and the ragged petals of dandelions and marigolds, scattered on her lap, showed that she had been trying to imitate the goldfish colour.

Hannah, as usual, was taking her illness seriously.

"Did you see a heron?" asked Robin, but there was no reply.

"Did you see a cannibal fish?" he continued, but there was silence.

"Did you see Mike Savage?" he asked, but though Hannah's lips moved monotonously, no sound came from them.

"I suppose you've got 'the dumbness'.—You can have it, then. I don't care!"

Robin began to count the goldfish. They were all there—swimming and flickering, gulping and gobbling—rising sometimes to snatch the ants' eggs scattered by Miss Armitage.

He thought that the biggest, which was paler than the others and had a bit out of its tail, looked even bigger than usual.

P'raps it is a cannibal fish, he thought, *or p'raps another cannibal fish tried to eat it and didn't like the taste of its tail or found it too big to swallow. Hannah may have seen something—something fishy. P'raps what she saw sent her dumb.*

"HANNAH!" he shouted, but the invalid scarecrow maintained her provoking silence.

Oh well, p'raps the fish nibbled its own tail like some people bite their nails. P'raps it's pale and big because it's overgrown its strength like Norma's mum says she has.

The fish and Hannah were dull company and Robin wandered towards the orchard. There could be no sleuthing this morning, because Mike Savage would not be working for Miss Armitage until the next day. Worzel

Gummidge, who was hatless, was standing beside Earthy Mangold under an old apple-tree.

"We come to look arter Hannah," explained Earthy. "We thought maybe if herons scared her we'd have to scare the herons arter all—terrible, long, pecky beaks herons has, and they might mistake Hannah's bootlace hair for eels and such-like wrigglers."

"I hope they do eat her hair," snapped Gummidge. "I hope they tugs it out savage. Maybe that'd stop her imitatin' me and sayin' she caught a illness."

"Sulks isn't a illness, Worzel, love—not a proper illness—not unless they lasts for ever. I happened to have a lady friend, her second name were Icy Crackle. Her first name *afore* her illness were Sunny Skewneck."

Here goes! thought Robin.

"She were called Sunny Skewneck acos her face an' neck was made from a sunflower head and stem—only a bit o' the stem; she weren't no taller nor me. She happened to work in the garden of a genelman as made ice-cream and rode it about on bicycles."

"He must've been daft! Stands to reason!" interrupted Gummidge.

"Maybe the ice-creams was restless and needed a change. Anyways, Sunny Skewneck worked in the genelman's gardin. She happened to a noticed as sunflowers twist their necks round and round so's they can look at the sun, so she twisted her neck all summer till it got stringy and her head dropped. By autumn there weren't much sun to look at, and she'd gone dizzy, so she let her head stay back to front and went into a sulk till the frost come and froze her hard. Her goldy petal hair turned white an' tinkled, but it were still a pretty frame for her face. Her legs an' arms was set in ice. The genelman's wife made a cake for Christmas and she told the childers she was goin' to ice it, an' make it look pretty. The childers was kind and helpful, so they thought they'd ice the cake for a surprise. They took it in the gardin an' left it there all night. It were froze lovely in the mornin'—all white an' sparklin' an' iced."

"But," interrupted Robin, "You don't ice a cake with *ice*. You ice it with sugar. That's what Mum does."

"Stands to reason she's daft!" said Worzel Gummidge rudely. "Ice ices."

"It do seem more sensible to ice with ice," agreed Earthy. "Maybe your Mum casn't think quite clear. Anyways, arter the cake were iced the childers happened to notice as Icy Crackle's face were the same size as the cake, an' they thought as how the petals of her hair'd look pretty set all round it, so they broke 'em off. She were too busy sulkin' to ask 'em to stop, so she ended bein' bald. It isn't safe to sulk all winter—nor all summer neither."

"Stand to reason sulkin's the safest thing there is. If worms sulked more and kept still they'd not be ate by thrushes. A sulkin' worm don't wriggle," said Gummidge.

"They do say as the early bird catches the worm—poor worm," remarked Earthy. "It's one o' those sayin's as Mrs Bloomsbury-Barton says."

"All sayin's as humans keeps on sayin' is daft!" declared Worzel Gummidge. "You've got to have an early worm for an early bird."

"Not if it's a glow-worm, Worzel, love. Glow-worms is for late-up birds." Earthy turned to Robin. "We was late-up last night. We walked over in the dark."

So Mike Savage had not brought the scarecrows to Miss Armitage's garden.

"It were then as Mr Gummidge were run over by a

moty car." Earthy spoke so casually that Robin did not think he could have heard her words correctly.

"He happened to be layin' down lookin' in a puddle an' the moty-car ran over him."

"Coo!" exclaimed Robin.

"I weren't run over." Gummidge spoke indignantly, "Stands to reason, I weren't run over. Moty-cars casn't run, they wheels."

"Then you was wheeled over, Worzel, love."

"I were *went* over. Wheels didn't touch me, acos I was layin' atween 'em, but the moty car stole me hat. Maybe someone in Lunnon's wearin' it now."

"Don't fret, Worzel, love. Marlene's gone off to get you a new hat."

Just then, Marlene came running into the orchard. She was carrying one of her greatest treasures—a policeman's battered helmet. Years ago, it had belonged to Constable Wilson, and when it had become too shabby for wear, Marlene had rescued it from a bonfire at the back of the Police Station. Robin looked on enviously as she popped the helmet on to the scarecrow's head. If only he, Robin, had a helmet, perhaps he could be a better detective. Some of the wisdom of the Police Force might have lingered in the helmet's crown. He wished he had a hat for Gummidge, but he owned no headgear except his red school cap, and a blue one for Sunday best. His mother would fuss if one of these was missing. He sighed as he thought how lucky were the grown-up detectives who could buy their own clothes and not have to obey their mothers.

"Don't Mr Gummidge look smart and handsome!" exclaimed Earthy admiringly.

Really, the scarecrow looked even more peculiar than

usual. His turnipy cheeks bulged under the narrow helmet, which had pushed a green sprout of his hair over his right eye.

"Ooh aye! I'm the best 'tecative hereabouts and I'll be the best 'tecative thereabouts. I've a mind to go to Lunnon and stand in the middle and scare the moty cars, and wait till I see my hat goin' by on the head of a smart genelman."

"That's a smashing idea!" said Robin, thinking that with Gummidge out of the way he could prove his own detecting powers. Foolishly, he added, "I'll be the Scatterbrook 'tec!"

It was foolish, because the scarecrow answered provokingly, "I'll 'tecative Scatterbrook first an' Lunnon arter!"

Even more foolishly because, by now, he should have learned not to argue with scarecrows, Robin boasted, "I'm going to sleuth Mike Savage, and I bet I'll cop him."

"Silly you are!" said Marlene. "Mike's O.K. Miss Armitage says he's a good prophet."

"What's that, love?" asked Earthy. "Beggin' your pardon, an' if it's all the same to you, an' not minding my iggerance."

Because he had been snubbed, Robin tried to show off his knowledge. "It's what you make when you buy a thing cheap and sell it dear—the bit in between's the profit."

Earthy furrowed her potato forehead as she tried to understand.

"Silly you are!" repeated Marlene, "Miss Armitage didn't mean *that*. She meant Mike's a prophet like the old men in Sunday School—Ezekiel and Jeremiah and—and the lot. Miss Armitage means Mike knows when things are going to happen—like they did."

Earthy looked even more puzzled as she murmured, "Upsidaisy says it's only childers as goes to Sunday School: she didn't happen to mention old genelmen with funny names."

"Of course they don't go to Sunday School. They died hundreds of years ago. They were in Bible history, and they knew what was going to happen."

Worzel Gummidge, smirking from below the blue helmet, said, "Stands to reason, anyone as is eddicate in histry knows what happened."

"But the prophets knew *before* it happened. Mike Savage knew the goldfish would disappear, so he's a prophet like the others."

"Don't talk so daft. The goldfish wasn't hatched hunerds o' years ago afore the old genelmen died."

Marlene shrugged her shoulders impatiently, and Worzel Gummidge continued to argue, "Anyone that's not daft or dumb can say a thing's goin' to happen when he knows it will."

"But nobody who's not a prophet can know a thing's going to happen before it happens." Marlene spoke snappishly.

"Stands to reason he can. If I demeaned mesel to be a prophet, I'd say 'Mrs Kibbins's tame duck'll gobble a pink worm as soon as the school bell starts ringin'—a great, big, fat, pink worm'. Then Mrs Kibbins's tame duck *would* gobble a great, big, fat, pink worm!"

"Oh, Worzel, love, how wunnderful you are!" exclaimed Earthy, and added, "Poor great, big, fat worm it'd need a deal o' comfortin'."

"But you couldn't know the duckling would swallow a worm just then," argued Robin. "You couldn't!"

"Stands to reason I'd know, acos I'd a caught a great

big, fat, pink worm an' hid it in my pocket, an' I'd give it to the duck soon as the school bell started ringin'. It'd be a daft duck as wouldn't gobble a great, big, fat, pink worm wrigglin' afore its beak. I'd be a prophet same as Mike Savage!"

"Silly you are!" said Marlene. (It was her new and most favourite expression.) "Silly you are!"

Robin said nothing, but he was thinking very hard indeed—*a prophet same as Mike Savage.* He turned the words over and over in his mind—*a prophet same as Mike Savage. A prophet*——

Before he could turn the words into clues, his thoughts were interrupted by Miss Armitage calling from the porch: "Robin! Marlene! Marlene! Robin!"

When the children reached her, she explained that she was going to bottle rhubarb to be sold at the village Produce Stall.

"I shall send the money to the R.S.P.C.A.," she explained. "I am sure you children will help me to wash the jars and cut the rhubarb. I shall do the bottling tomorrow in the old wash-house."

So, while the white kittens played round their feet, Robin and Marlene cut rhubarb stems into lengths and washed and polished dozens of big bottling jars.

"There!" said Miss Armitage as she unwrapped a kitten that had folded itself into a rhubarb leaf. "There! That's a splendid morning's work! I shall begin the bottling first thing tomorrow morning. Mike won't be here, so I shall have the wash-house to myself."

There were, as the children discovered, many other things to do next morning, which was Saturday. Because it was market day, Marlene and her mother went by the early bus to Dimden. As soon as his seven o'clock breakfast was over, Robin decided to visit the scarecrows.

Hannah Harrow had left or been moved from her deck-chair by the goldfish pond, and Worzel Gummidge had taken her place. He lolled, broomstick legs stuck straight out in front of him, policeman's helmet hiding half his face, turnip lips pouting in slumber or sulks.

"Hullo!" said Robin perkily.

It was a perky sort of morning. Buds were bursting for joy and excitement. Spiders had been busy on the dewy grass and little white clouds were chasing one another across a blue, blue sky. Only the scarecrow did not share in the gladness of the morning.

"Hullo!" said Robin again.

There was no answer—not even the faintest rustle from Worzel Gummidge's straw stomach.

"Heck!" muttered Robin, who was feeling companion-able.

The concrete surrounding the goldfish pond was heavily splashed and rather muddy.

A heron? wondered Robin and he peered down into the pool. So far as he could see, it was not nearly so full of fish as it had been yesterday, and the ones who were left were darting about more rapidly than usual.

Cannibal fish? wondered Robin. *But why would a cannibal fish make muddy splashes? If it* IS *a cannibal, I bet it's that big pale one with the chip out of its tail.*

He lay down on the wet concrete, shaded his eyes from the sun and stared down into the pool.

THE BIG PALE GOLDFISH WAS NOT THERE.

But something—a golden brown, rather fish-shaped something *was* there. Robin stared again. Yes, the some-thing was a bottle-straw boot, and a few loose straws were floating in the water.

"Gimme me smart boot!" shouted Worzel Gummidge.

As he stood up, Robin saw that the right ankle of the scarecrow was bare, and he noticed something else that he had not noticed before—drops were dripping from his helmet and the dark blue stuff that covered it was almost black, because it was sodden with water.

"What's your bottle-straw boot doing in the pool?" he asked stupidly.

"It's not doin' nothin' that I knows of, not NOW!" replied Gummidge. "It were bein' a fish-chaser—same as me helmet were bein' a fish-catcher. Folks did ought to be scared o' the perlice, seeing as perlice is human-scarers. I started bein' perlice soon as I was give a perlice hat."

"That didn't make you a policeman," argued Robin.

"Stands to reason, it did. Hats is the only way humans can tell humans from t'other humans—there's soldiers' hats and perlicemen's hats and postman's hats and bonnets for babies and shawls for gipsies and crowns for queens. How'd you tell a postman from a baby if they wasn't wearin' differ hats?"

"By the pram, of course."

"They mightn't be wearin' prams!" said Worzel Gummidge triumphantly.

Before Robin could answer, kind Miss Armitage came scurrying towards the pool. "I've been burgled!" she said. "It's a bad burglary. Oh! Thank goodness the policeman is here!"

Worzel Gummidge smirked proudly as Miss Armitage addressed him.

"Constable," she said. "Constable, how good of you to come so promptly. But how did you know?"

Gummidge's grin spread so widely that it almost met

the curving brim of his helmet, and his stomach rustled proudly.

"Constable!" repeated Miss Armitage.

Her voice changed as she walked nearer to the pool—"But it isn't the policeman: it's a—it's only a scarecrow."

Instantly, Worzel Gummidge's face stiffened into sulkiness, so that, except for his helmet, he looked a very ordinary scarecrow.

"Mike Savage must have put it there in place of the other scarecrow," continued Miss Armitage. "How very clever and thoughtful of him. He said the herons would get used to the other scarecrow. I suppose he thought a change would baffle them. Now I must telephone to the Police Station."

"What's been burgled?" asked Robin.

"All the white kittens, and yet the wash-house door was locked, and the key was in its usual hiding-place. Come, and I'll show you."

Now I can be a proper 'tec, thought Robin as he followed Miss Armitage, *I'll look for clues and finger-prints and footmarks.*

There *were* footmarks on a patch of overturned soot on the wash-house floor, but they were not human ones: they were the soft little paddy prints of kittens' paws. All the same, Robin felt like a big-game tracker as he knelt down to examine these clues.

The cardboard carton was tipped on its side and a mound of the spilled soot was sprinkled with little white hairs.

Suddenly, Robin noticed a most exciting clue on one of the flaps of the carton, and pointed to it.

"Blood!" he yelled, "there's a thumb-mark in blood! Look!"

Miss Armitage, who had been kneeling by the fireplace and peering up the chimney, gave a distressed yelp and jumped to her feet.

"Where? Oh, I do hope the burglar didn't wound the kittens, poor little things!"

"It's a red *thumb* mark—not a red *paw* print!" Robin told her. "So the kittens must have scratched the burglar—scratched him hard. There are drops of blood on the floor, look!" He felt tremendously important as he followed the trail of little red spots leading from the carton to a table where a row of glass jars stood ready for the rhubarb bottling.

"Six, twelve, eighteen." Miss Armitage was counting aloud. "Twenty. Four of the jars are missing. I know we washed two dozen yesterday. Who would want to steal four bottling jars and five white kittens—sweet though the kittens are? I had wondered if the poor little things could have scrambled up the chimney. But *jars* couldn't have climbed the chimney. I must go and telephone to the policeman. I hope he's at home, but it may be his Dimden day."

Robin hardly heard what she was saying. He was staring at the remains of a ball of yellow string, staring particularly at the loose end which was stained with blood. There was a small splash of blood on the table, too.

As soon as he was alone, he prowled round the wash-house and hunted for more clues. There was a grimy paw print on a table leg, and two more on one of the white-washed walls. There was a tiny tuft of grey fur and a few single hairs, also grey, caught in a slit of the table-top.

I suppose I'd better leave these clues till the copper's been, thought Robin. *That burglar must've had grey hair and he must've caught his head against the edge of the table, so he can't be Mike, because Mike's got black hair. All we've got to do's to find a grey-haired man with a wounded thumb. Then we'll match his thumb-print with the one on the flap of the carton, and Bob's your uncle! Oh, and the burglar may've tied up his thumb with yellow string. His prints'll be on the key, too. P'raps he's a buddy of Mike's, or how'd he know the key was hidden under a flower-pot by the wash-house door? Heck! It looks like an inside job, but nobody lives inside the house—only Miss Armitage.*

He was puzzling over the problems when Miss Armitage bustled into the wash-house.

"It's too tiresome!" she said. "The policeman *is* in Dimden. I'll go and see him there, and explain things personally. You can come, too, if you like. We shall have time to catch the ten-thirty bus. We'll take the cat basket with us. I should like to buy some tortoises in the market. I can't bear the way the poor things are all huddled together in that cage with no soft grass. Wait here, and I'll get the basket."

"Can I have that bit of yellow string?" asked Robin.

"Yes, dear, of course—anything you like. I'm so worried about those poor kittens. I hope they're happy wherever they are!"

Miss Armitage bustled away, and Robin helped himself to clues. By the time she returned, his pockets were bulging with yellow string, blood-stained cardboard, grey hairs (wrapped in a toffee paper), white hairs and soot (in an envelope which had held his Aunt Mabel's birthday card) and the wash-house key with its blue label (folded very carefully into his own handkerchief, which he had used as a painting rag).

"Now!" said Miss Armitage.

The engine of the Dimden bus seemed to be doing its

very best to help as it chugged up the hill—*Mike Savage! Mike Savage! Mike Savage! Mike Savage! Mike Savage!*

Wrong clue, chum! thought Robin.

The bus drew up by the side of the Market Square. The usual crowd of people was gathered round the Pet Stall, where canaries and budgerigars were crowded into too small cages, where guinea-pigs and rabbits lurked in hutches, where puppies yelped frantically, kittens washed their faces and goldfish, in tiny bowls, gulped as gloomily as Hannah Harrow.

"I should like to buy them all!" exclaimed Miss Armitage. "But we came to look for tortoises."

She began to push her way through the little crowd, and Robin followed till he was separated from her by a woman who was carrying a parrot in a cage.

"Please let me have it, Mum!"

Robin recognised Marlene's voice, though he could not see her. Another voice (it belonged to the Pet Stall man) spoke: "It's a pure grey Persian kitten, ducks, worth every penny of half a crown. It'd cost a guinea any day in London. A gentleman brought five of them in this morning. It breaks me heart to part with them. They'll be gone in a brace of shakes."

Other voices chimed in:

"First grey Persian ever I've seen with a pink nose!"

"Persian, my foot!"

"There's one in the cage with white paws and ears! Call that a grey Persian, do you?"

"Their mum was a white Persian" (this from the Pet Stall man). "These kittens are special!"

Now Marlene's mother was speaking: "Give the kitten back, Marl, there's a good girl. The filthy little thing's made your new blue coat as black as soot."

The kitten mewed protestingly. Robin, trying to hustle forward, was pushed and jostled until he came almost face to face with a large pale goldfish, bumping its nose against the glass of its bowl, and looking sadly at the world outside. It gulped gloomily, and as it flicked round, Robin saw that a piece was missing from its tail. There was no doubt that it was one of the fish from Miss Armitage's pool!

Before he could think what to do, he was hustled sideways until he found himself opposite to a wire-fronted box. In it were four rather queer-looking kittens. Their coats were grimy grey and their noses were pink. One had two white paws, one had an almost white face, one was washing its ears, and one, gripping its tail between two paws, was licking the tip of its tail. They were washing themselves as their mother had taught them, and doing it very thoroughly. As Robin watched, the tip of a tail whitened and an ear turned to paler grey.

Marlene, clutching a fifth kitten to what had been a pale blue coat, was arguing with her mother: "Do let me have it. It's ever so pretty. It won't be dirty when I've brushed it!"

Robin edged closer, said, "Let's have a look!" and snatched the kitten from her grimy hands.

"It's made your face all dirty, too!" protested Marlene's mother. "You shouldn't go kissing strange kittens. You don't know where they've come from!"

But Robin thought he knew! Darting forward, he snatched his handkerchief out of his pocket and dipped it into a goldfish bowl. There was a chinking of metal against glass as Miss Armitage's wash-house key slid into the bowl, smashing it to smithereens. Out skidded the big pale goldfish, and the Pet Stall man shouted, "What do you think you're doing?"

"What do you think you're doing?" shouted the Pet Stall man

Robin, thankful for the pause while the fish was being scooped up and popped into another bowl, knew exactly what he was doing: he was washing a kitten, and turning it from grey to very nearly white. The smell of soot tickled his nose. The wet handkerchief turned blacker and blacker as the kitten, showing a very clean pink tongue, mewed pathetically. Before the little creature was quite white, Robin felt himself seized by the collar and shaken.

"Haven't you done enough damage without trying to half drown the kitten?" asked the Pet Stall man. "I've a good mind to fetch the police. Pedigree kittens are delicate."

"It's *our* kitten," Robin answered jerkily between shakes. "It's—our kitten and—it's not—grey Persian—it's white. The goldfish are—ours, too."

"A likely story!"

The Pet Stall man gave Robin an even harder shake, and then Miss Armitage, who knew nothing of what had happened, hurried to the rescue. Like many small and mild-looking people, she could be very fierce sometimes, so when she cried, "Leave that little boy alone *at once*," the Pet Stall man took his huge hand from Robin's collar.

The explanations that followed were puzzling to the little crowd, and not very clear to Miss Armitage.

"He *greyed* them with soot!" said Robin. "He did it for disguise."

"I never did!" muttered the Pet Stall man.

"He left white hairs in the soot in the wash-house. I've got a lot of clues—a thumb-print and yellow string with blood on it. Look!"

Robin handed the kitten to Marlene, who clutched it tenderly—adding damp to her coat and more soot to the kitten.

"Look!" Robin pulled his clues out of his pockets and

waved them triumphantly. "And *there's* the key by the smashed bowl, and *there's* the cannibal goldfish in another bowl. I knew it by the bit out of its tail and because it's so pale. I bet all the other fish are ours, too."

"I *said* grey Persians don't have pink noses!" put in a voice from the crowd.

Miss Armitage, looking from one to another, murmured, "I don't *quite* understand."

"Nor anyone else neither!" snarled the Pet Stall man. "Only this young hooligan's smashed a valuable goldfish bowl, and now he's trying to make out the kittens are his."

"Miss Armitage's," corrected Marlene.

"I don't know whose they were to start with," the man spoke surlily. "All I know is the kittens and the fish were brought to us by a gentleman who supplies us regular."

"What's his name?" asked Robin. "Is it Mike Savage?"

"Oh, surely not!" Miss Armitage sounded dreadfully distressed. "Surely not Mike Savage?"

"How should I know his name? You can ask him yourself if you wait. He'll be back any time now to collect his jars—he brings the fish in Kilner jars—and get his money. I hadn't the cash when we opened this morning."

A woman stepped forward and asked to see a kitten.

"I think," said Miss Armitage firmly, "I think I had better look at the kittens first."

She moved towards their cage and peeped inside.

Even from where he stood, Robin could see that the kittens' washing had been successful; ears and paws and faces were much whiter.

"Yes," Miss Armitage straightened herself, "yes, these kittens were stolen from me. The smallest has one blue eye and one green: *my* smallest kitten had a blue eye and a green eye."

Heck! thought Robin. *Heck! I never noticed, and I thought I'd all the clues.*

"There's the chap!" exclaimed the Pet Stall man. "There he is, picking up his jars from behind the stall. I'll have a word with him. *Then* p'raps you'll all be satisfied."

He edged round the stall and Robin followed. A moment later, he felt as though he had reached the end of a beautiful dream that had become suddenly true. Mike Savage had collected the jars; they dangled from yellow strings. His right thumb was bandaged with a grimy rag.

"Take his thumb prints!" shouted Robin, waving the blood-stained cardboard. "I bet it'll match this one. The string matches, too!"

With a most satisfying crash, the jars broke on the pavement. Mike Savage snatched his bicycle that had been propped against a corner of the stall, and rattled away over the cobblestones.

"Oh dear!" sighed Miss Armitage who, with Marlene, had followed Robin. "Oh dear, it does seem a pity, and he seemed such a good, kind man."

"Shame to think we washed and polished that lot!" Marlene looked complainingly at the broken glass.

"Reckon we shan't see that man again in a hurry!" The Pet Stall man turned to Miss Armitage. "I'm sorry about this, Miss, and I'd not've shook the little chap if I'd known. Still, shaking breaks no bones, does it, lad?"

It was Robin's turn to shake his own head. At the moment he felt that the joy of having been an *almost* first-class detective could make up for at least a dozen broken bones.

"Shall we go to the Police Station now?" he asked hopefully for he longed to show his clues.

"No call for that," said the Pet Stall man. Perhaps he

thought that Robin wanted to make a complaint about the shaking. "No call for that. Tell you what, would you like a puppy? I've a real little beauty—a spaniel that's just begging for a good home."

The puppy was a beauty—jet black all over except for his teeth, which were as white as snowdrops, and his tongue, which was as rosy as a rose.

The Pet Stall man explained that he was not going to sell any more puppies in the market. That pleased Miss Armitage as much as his wriggling, loving, flop-eared present delighted Robin.

"It's more like a Noah's Ark than a bus!" remarked Marlene an hour later. She was clutching her kitten because she had won the battle with her mother. Robin was nursing his puppy. The seat beside him was shared by Miss Armitage, four kittens in the cat basket and two bewildered-looking tortoises in a box. In a borrowed tank, half filled with water, goldfish swam lazily, bumping into one another as the bus lurched round corners on the way to Scatterbrook.

I'll call the pup Tracker, thought Robin, *I'll teach him to be a tracker dog. No, p'raps I'll call him 'Tec.*

"Tracker!" he whispered, and the puppy wagged his stump of a tail in wild delight.

" 'Tec!" whispered Robin, and a pink tongue licked his hand, a tail wagged and a black body quivered for joy.

"I'll give him a blue collar."

"Pink's prettier," mused Marlene. "I'll call my kitty Pinky after his pink nose."

"Pink's for a girl!" Robin spoke scornfully, "Blue's for a boy. Blue's for the police and Tracker-Tec's going to be a police dog when I'm the best 'tec of Scotland Yard."

"Red's smarter—red'd show up against his black coat."

And red's the colour of blood, thought Robin, *and blood gave me two of my clues.*

The tortoises weaved their skinny necks from side to side, the goldfish golluped gloomily, the kitten purred and the puppy licked Robin's face as the bus slurred to a stop in Scatterbrook.

Two or three hours later, when Miss Armitage was resting, and Marlene's kitten was as white as snow and her coat was being washed by her mother (Marlene's coat—not the kitten's!), and when Robin's father was buying a *yellow* collar for the puppy and when the goldfish were at home in their pool, Robin went to visit his scarecrow friends. The deck-chair was empty and a sodden bottle-straw, fished out of the pool by kind Miss Armitage, lay beside it.

"Gummidge will want his boot," remarked Robin to the large pale goldfish and, picking up the bottle-straw, he hurried towards the shrubbery.

There, happy in their freedom, the two tortoises were tearing at a clump of dandelion leaves. Staring down at them were three scarecrows—Hannah Harrow, who lolled saggingly against a tree stump, Worzel Gummidge, whose right ankle was imbedded in a heap of leaf mould, and Earthy Mangold, who was speaking crooningly: "Oh, things, loves—you'll need a deal o' comfortin'."

"They're rabbits gone hard!" moaned Hannah. "It's only rabbits as eats dandylions."

"They're birds!" announced Gummidge. "They've beaks like birds."

"They're snails!" declared Earthy, "They're snails

gone sad and hard and needin' comfortin'. They've shells like snails—same colour, same patches."

"Snails has horns same as cows," argued Gummidge.

"But more jellified, love. Snails' horns goes in and out; cows' horns stays hard for proddin'. These things, loves, puts me in mind o' a lady friend I knew. She happened to have a jellified stummick, acos her stummick happened to be made from a jelly-bag with the blackberry juice squeezed out, so she took a fancy to harden her stummick and went an' lay in a path o' wet concrete. She only turned from front to back just in time, but she were never quite the same again, acos her back legs was too spindly to bear her weight without help from her poor arms. She were called Minnie Four Legs arter that, an' her back was as hard as her stummick an' she used her arms for legs."

The tortoises waved their sad heads, and their beakish faces showed no interest at all as Earthy continued: "I casn't abear to think what'll happen when these things-loves has famlies o' little things-loves that'll need to nestle up to soft stummicks for comfortin'."

Robin broke into the conversation, and announced, "They lay eggs!"

"I told you they was birds." Gummidge sounded triumphant.

"They're reptiles, I think." Robin could not resist showing off his knowledge. "Reptiles are snakes, sort of."

Hannah Harrow sagged shudderingly, and moaned, "Snakes is long an' wriggling an' squirms at you. Maybe these has long, squirming wriggles packed inside their shells. Squirmy wriggles is infectious."

"I happened to have a lady friend o' the name o' Connie Squirmy-Wriggle," put in Earthy. "She were called that acos her body happened to be made from an old concertina. Her mouth were a mouth-organ, acos she worked for a music genelman. She musicked when the wind blew fierce through her teeth—very sad she musicked——"

Robin, feeling it was time to change the subject, because he was not in the mood to listen to a long story, interrupted "We caught Mike Savage. I found some smashing clues and *I* caught him. He'd pinched the kittens and the goldfish——"

"They must a needed comfortin'," put in Earthy. "It's not nice nor kind to pinch poor little soft kitten-loves, and I casn't see how nobody could pinch goldfish—they're so skiddy."

"I mean he stole them, and *I* was the 'tec and found them."

"Stands to reason I were the 'tecative!" boasted Gummidge.

"You weren't! You didn't find any clues."

"I'd not demean mesel to go daftin' about arter clues not when I'd seed Mike Savage fillin' jars with goldfish when I were sittin' by the pool."

"Then why didn't you stop him?" demanded Robin.

"Acos I were sulkin'. Stands to reason I were sulkin' same as any perlice 'tecative'd sulk if his hat were bein' used as a fishin' net and his best boot as a goldfish-chaser!"

"You might have told me!" Robin flung the bottle-straw boot towards Gummidge.

"I did happen to remark as my boot were a fish-chaser."

It was true, maddeningly true, and Robin had missed that particular clue. He kicked at a tree trunk and stubbed his toe, while the tortoises looked enquiringly upwards.

"Asides," continued Gummidge, "asides you likes to

'tecative roundabout an' complicate. If I sees a thrush peepin' down the wrong worm-hole, I doesn't demean mesel to interfere. Same if I seed a bull tossin' the wrong farmer I'd let it go on bein' roundabout an' complicate an' wearin' out its horns on the wrong farmer till it found the right one."

"Poor farmer-loves!" murmured Earthy.

"Bulls needs their fun same as farmers—the longer the fun the funnier 'tis. Robin likes bein' roundabout an' complicate same as I likes bein' the best 'tecative hereabouts!"

One of the tortoises ambled towards Hannah and pushed its sad and elderly face against her.

With a shrill scream, she struggled upwards and walked droopingly away. Earthy followed, Gummidge pushed the end of his right broomstick into his bottle-straw boot, prodded the tortoise, and said, "I'm goin' back to Ten Acre. I'll not demean mesel to stay along o' things as don't know if they're birds or snails or adders or rabbits."

As the "best 'tecative" of Scatterbrook shambled away, Robin remembered his own happiness. He had a ship in a bottle, and the ship had magic to send his mind voyaging round the world into secret harbours, to desert islands and across (the words of a poem, learned at school, jumped into his mind) "perilous seas." He had an even greater treasure—a pink-tongued, white-toothed, floppy-eared, wriggling, loving treasure of a puppy.

He was so rich that he could be generous, so he shouted across the shrubbery, "O.K., Worzel Gummidge. I'll *let* you be the best 'tec hereabouts."

A dark blue helmet nodded between the trees, and the scarecrow's rusty voice answered, "Ooh aye! Stands to reason!"